Early ure

Early Christian Art and Architecture

An Introduction

Guntram Koch

SCM PRESS LTD

Translated by John Bowden from the German
Frühchristliche Kunst. Eine Einführung,
published 1995 by W. Kohlhammer Gmbh,
Stuttgart, Berlin and Cologne 1995.

0 334 02632 6

First British edition published 1996
by SCM Press Ltd,
9–17 St Albans Place, London N1 0NX

Typeset at The Spartan Press Ltd,
Lymington, Hants
and printed in Great Britain by
Biddles Ltd, Guildford and King's Lynn

Contents

I

General

1. Introduction

The centuries between 200 and 600 CE are known as late antiquity or the early Christian period. This is one of the most fascinating eras of world history, which in art had an influence down to the nineteenth century and in some respects is stilll influential today. The inherited tradition, that of Graeco-Roman art, was given new content, adapted to new needs and in this way 'Christianized'. A Christian art came about through the reinterpretation and transformation of Graeco-Roman art. Here are some examples.

In the fourth century the basilica was the predominant form for church buildings. Its predecessor was the Roman market basilica; the type was transformed to some degree by Christians for their new purposes and provided with the decorations and furnishings necessary for worship. In the West the basilica – of course with changes – remained for centuries the preferred type of building. When we look at, to give just a few examples, St Michael in Hildesheim (1003–1033), the monastic church in Alpirsbach (c.1100) or the Peace Church in Potsdam (1845–1854), we should remember that this type goes back to the early Christian period.

The use of centralized forms for churches also has its origin in early Christian times. One need only recall the Palatine Chapel in Aachen (c.800) and subsequent buildings there, or St Michael in Fulda (820–822 and the beginning of the eleventh century) and other 'copies' of the rotunda of the Church of the Holy Sepulchre in Jerusalem.

In 320 CE the first monastery was built by Pachomius in Tabenissi in Upper Egypt. After that, monasticism spread first in the Eastern empire, and then in the West. After the founding of Montecassino (c.530) by Benedict of Nursia (c.480–555/60) and the Rule which

he composed, along with the activity of Cassiodorus (died after 580),
it flourished greatly there. In the Middle Ages the monasteries in
Europe were to become extremely significant as centres of art,
culture and science.

The Christian world of graphic art arose after the third century
CE. Pagan motives were taken over and 'Christianized'. For
example, the seated Isis with the boy Horus became Mary with her
child; bearded father deities (Zeus, Asclepius, Poseidon) became
the bearded Christ; the embodiment of one of the seasons became
the youthful Christ; the sleeping Endymion became Jonah asleep in
the boat; a warrior brandishing a sword became Abraham intent on
killing Isaac. Examples could be continued almost indefinitely.

When we admire wall paintings in mediaeval and later churches,
we should remember that we have early Christianity to thank for
providing wall paintings and mosaics to decorate the interiors of
churches. At the beginning of the extant examples stand the
paintings in the baptistery of Dura Europos, which were probably
done in 232/233 CE.

In the early Christian period it also became customary to provide
biblical manuscripts with illustrations; to make pictures of Christ,
Mary and the saints and of events from the Old and New
Testaments; to use ivory for small tablets, chests and boxes; to make
fabrics depicting Christian scenes and to use silver for liturgical
objects. The Middle Ages took this up.

So the early Christian period had a quite decisive significance for
later centuries in the spheres of architecture, graphic art, iconography and art on a smaller scale.

2. Chronology and geographical distribution –
division into phases

Christianity originated in Palestine, i.e. in the east of the Roman
empire. Already in the first century it spread not only in the
provinces of the Near East but also westwards, and increasingly so in
the second century. In the third century there were Christian
communities in numerous cities throughout the Roman empire, and
Christianity also penetrated into the countryside. During this period

Christians were at best tolerated and sometimes also cruelly persecuted, but a complete change took place under Constantine the Great, whose edicts of 311 and 313 officially made Christianity a legitimate religion and one which was even preferred, as a result of the personal involvement of the emperor.

So early Christian art can be found in all the regions of the Roman empire, from Britain, Gaul, Spain and North Africa in the West to Asia Minor, Syria, Palestine, Arabia and Egypt in the East, and in addition in areas which had not been conquered by Rome at all or occupied by Romans only for a short period. These include Nubia (in the Sudan), Ethiopia, Mesopotamia (Iraq), the island of Khark in the Persian Gulf, Armenia, Georgia, the Crimea and Ireland. This introduction concentrates on the central areas; the significant 'Coptic' art of Egypt is only mentioned by way of exception; it really needs separate treatment (see the bibliography in 5 below).

As far as we know, early Christian art begins around 200. So far no fragments have been found from an earlier period, and literary sources suggest that they are hardly to be expected. However, anyone who wants to consider the early Christian period in depth must take into account the earlier periods, at least the Roman imperial period of the first three centuries CE. For early Christian art is part of Roman – or even Graeco-Roman – art, and it is only natural to bear earlier artistic creations in mind.

It is more difficult to fix a lower chronological limit. In the provinces of the East, i.e. Egypt, Arabia, Palestine and Syria, and also in North Africa and Spain, the conquest by the Islamic Arabs after 635 CE marks a deep break and the end of early Christian art. However, Syria and Palestine had already been ravaged early in the seventh century by the invasions of the Sassanids (Persians), so no artistic evidence has survived from this time. In Constantinople and within its sphere of influence (above all Asia Minor and the Balkans), a new development can be established under the emperor Justinian (who reigned from 527–565), so the end of the early Christian phase there is to be put at 530 CE. The middle of the sixth century should also be taken as the limit for the Balkans, since the area was then devastated by the invasions of the Slavs. In Italy the conquest by the Langobards (568 and after) and the pontificate of Pope Gregory the Great (590–604) mark a break.

The time-span from around 200 to around 600 CE can be sub-divided into several phases. However, the difficulty is that some of these only apply to certain areas and do not figure at all in others, and some phases only become clear in connection with particular genres of art, and not with others. So here a division into three phases is proposed, though it will only be applied where it seems meaningful; a more marked – or a rather different – sub-division is possible with different genres (e.g. with sarcophagi):

– before Constantine (c.200–311/313);
– the time of Constantine (311/313 – 337/361);
– after Constantine (337/362 –c.550/600).

3. Some historical dates

The history of late antiquity is very confused. There were countless emperors, sometimes one main emperor and several co-emperors, and in addition usurpers who had seized the throne illegally. Wars were necessary on almost all the frontiers to safeguard the ongoing existence of the empire. Many 'barbarian peoples', almost too many to number, invaded imperial territory. The exact circumstances cannot be elucidated here; however, some dates may serve as a background for early Christian art.

c.30	Jesus dies in Jerusalem on the cross
48/50	Paul's missionary journey to Antioch; 'Apostolic Council' in Jerusalem
c.50	Paul founds a community in Corinth; beginning of the expansion of Christianity in the Mediterranean, also among 'Gentiles' (not just among Jews)
64	Conflagration in Rome; Christians are accused; first persecution; martyrdom of Peter (?)
c.67	Martyrdom of Paul in Rome
2nd century	Increasing expansion of Christianity
c.200	Bishop Zephyrinus of Rome (197–217) entrusts the deacon Calixtus (later to be his successor) with the administration of a cemetery for the community on the Via Appia, probably the present-day Catacombs of St Calixtus; this marks the beginning of the

	building of the catacombs and their decoration with paintings
c.215	Clement of Alexandria dies
c.160–220	Tertullian of Carthage
232/233	Conversion of a private house in Dura Europos, Syria, into a 'house church' (it was destroyed in 256); the earliest extant church (paintings in the baptistery)
250	Persecution of Christians under the emperor Decius (249–251)
Middle of 3rd century	Christians have increased substantially in number in large areas of the empire; for example, it is estimated that there were between 15,000 and 20,000 Christians in Rome
257	Persecution of Christians under the emperor Valentinian (253–260); after this there were forty years of peaceful development and expansion
c.280	Armenia is Christianized by Gregory the Illuminator
286	Emperor Diocletian nominates Maximianus Herculius 'Augustus' of the West, thus dividing the empire into two parts
293	Establishment of the 'tetrarchy' ('rule of four') by Diocletian; he became 'Augustus' of the East (with his residence in Nicomedia); Galerius was 'Caesar' of the East (residing in Thessalonica and Sirmium); Maximus became 'Augustus of the West' (with his residence in Milan and Aquileia); and Constantius Chlorus 'Caesar' of the West (with residences in Trier and York); among other developments, palaces were built in the cities
303–5	Persecution of Christians under Diocletian, predominantly in the east of the Empire
305	'Second tetrarchy' with Galerius as Augustus and Maximinus Daia as Caesar in the East, and Constantius Chlorus as Augustus and Severus as Caesar in the West
306	Constantius Chlorus dies; his son Constantine is proclaimed Augustus by the army; in Rome Maxentius, son of Maximian, becomes emperor; Constantine prefers to live in Trier (where he builds his residence) and strives for mastery in Rome
311	Galerius, Licinius and Constantine decree an act of

	toleration for Christians and the Christian religion becomes a *religio licita* (permitted religion)
312	Constantine with his troops (bearing the *labarum* on their standards and shields) defeats Maxentius at the Milvian Bridge and thus becomes sole ruler in the West
313	Constantine and Licinius, the Augustus of the East, agree in Milan to allow Christianity as a permitted religion throughout the empire ('Edict of Milan')
313–324	Constantine is Augustus in the West; he founds a large number of churches in Rome and in other places in Italy and North Africa, most of which are richly decorated
313–324	Licinius is Augustus in the East
324	Constantine defeats Licinius and thus becomes sole ruler of the whole empire; the 'foundation' of Byzantium as the 'New Rome' (Constantinople); the beginning of the expansion and development of the city with new walls, a forum and churches
320/325	Pachomius (c.287–342/346) founds the first monastery in Tabenissi in Upper Egypt
325	First Ecumenical Council in Nicaea
326	Helena, Constantine's mother, travels in the Holy Land; Constantine founds churches in the holy places in Jerusalem, Bethlehem and Mamre and in Baalbek and Antioch
330	Inauguration of Constantinople and the transfer of the seat of imperial government
333	An anonymous pilgrim from Bordeaux travels through the Holy Land and writes a report which also gives information about the buildings; the beginning of pilgrim literature
260/265–339	Eusebius, Bishop of Caesarea (in Palestine) from 313, author of a *History of the Church* and a *Life of Constantine*, also important sources for early Christian art
337	Death of Constantine the Great (he was baptized on his deathbed)
337–361	Rule of Constantine's sons: Constantine II (337–340), Constans (337–350) and Constantius II (337–361); various anti-emperors

From the middle of the 4th century	Milan becomes the preferred imperial residence in Italy; the palace is extended and churches are built
355	Franks cross the Rhine and capture Cologne; the Rhine frontier is again restored by the Romans
361–363	The emperor Julian (Julian the Apostate or Julian the Philosopher), the last supporter of the old Roman religion, attempts to take action against the Christians
Above all the second half of the 4th century	Activity of the 'church fathers' Basil of Caesarea (in Cappadocia, 330–379, important as the founder of Greek monasticism); Gregory of Nyssa (c.335–394); Gregory of Nazianzus (died 390); John Chrysostom (c.350–407), for a while Patriarch of Constantinople; Ambrose of Milan (c.339–397), from 374 Bishop of Milan
364–375	Valentinian I emperor in the West; for a time resides in Trier (palace built, villa in Konz); his brother Valens 364–378 in the East
375–383	Sons of Valentinian I, Gratian (375–383) emperor in the West (Gaul) and Valentinian II similarly emperor in the West (Italy)
c.375	Beginning of the 'migrations', including Germanic military campaigns against the Roman empire, after the invasion of the Huns from Asia
379–395	Theodosius I emperor in the East, nominated by Gratian; heyday of art ('Theodosian renaissance')
379/380	Gratian and then Theodosius prescribe the 'Catholic' faith
381	Gratian forbids 'pagan' sacrifices and in 383 (?) abolishes the office of Pontifex Maximus
391	Theodosius I prohibits pagan cults; Christianity becomes the state religion
393	Last Olympic Games
395	After the death of Theodosius I the empire is divided under his sons Arcadius and Honorius
395–408	Arcadius emperor in the East
395–423	Honorius emperor in the West
401	Roman troops withdrawn from the Rhine frontier
402	Transfer of the capital in the West from Milan to Ravenna; the city flourishes and there is lively building activity
408–450	Theodosius II emperor in the East (son of Arcadius):

considerable building activity, including the expansion of Constantinople and the building of a new city wall

First half of 5th century
Germans (Arians) penetrate the western parts of imperial territory in large numbers and found states there: the kingdoms of the Burgundians, the West Goths on the Spanish peninsula, the East Goths in Italy and the Vandals in North Africa become particularly important

410
Goths under Alaric capture Rome

431
Third Ecumenical Council in Ephesus: Mary is recognized as Mother of God (Theotokos)

451
Fourth Ecumenical Council in Chalcedon

474/5 and 476–91
Zeno emperor in Constantinople; buildings in the East (Qalat Siman, Meriamlik)

476
End of the Western Roman empire; the German (Thuringian) Odovacar deposes Romulus Augustulus and becomes king of Italy (476–493)

493–526
Theoderic, an East Goth (Arian), king in Italy, with the toleration of the emperor in Constantinople; capital Ravenna; buildings for the Arians

496/497
Baptism of Clovis (Catholic), king of the Franks (482–511), who had founded a great kingdom in Gaul and Germania; this gives the Pope new support

527–565
Justinian I emperor of the Roman empire; partial reconquest of territories lost to the Germans (Italy, North Africa, parts of Spain); grandiose building activity and blossoming of the arts; increased separation of the West in the development of style. Beginning of the early 'Byzantine' period

529
The Academy in Athens closed

c.530
Benedict of Nursia (c.480–555/60) founds the monastery of Montecassino; his rule is a decisive influence on Western monasticism

From middle of 6th century
Slavs invade the Balkans and cause considerable devastation

568–574
Langobards (Germans) conquer Italy (there is a Langobard kingdom there until 774, capital Pavia)

590–604
Gregory I (the Great) Pope in Rome: separates the papacy from the emperor and patriarch in Constantinople; mission to the Anglo-Saxons and Langobards;

	fourth Latin 'church father' after Ambrose, Jerome and Augustine
Beginning of 7th century	Sassanids (Persians) invade Syria and Palestine; land devastated
622	Flight of Muhammad from Mecca to Medina (*hijra*); beginning of the expansion of Islam
632	Death of Muhammad
after 634	Arabs conquer Palestine and Syria (636), Jerusalem (638), Iraq (637), Egypt (639–641), Persia (to 657), North Africa (643–697), and large parts of the Spanish peninsula (711–716), the Roman empire thus loses enormous areas

4. History of research

Interest in the art works of late antiquity, with 'Christian archaeology', began around the middle of the sixteenth century in Rome, and of course Roman monuments were at its centre. This was not an investigation of antiquarian detail or even a history of art. Rather, Counter-Reformers and Post-Reformers attempted to derive arguments for the correctness of their beliefs from monuments of the early Christian period.

Important authors and publications from the early period are as follows. A. Fulvio in a five-volume work *Antiquitates Urbis*, Rome 1527, describes the catacombs in Vol.IV and the other early Christian monuments in Vol.V, but there are no illustrations. The great work by A. Bosio (1575–1629), *Roma sotterranea* (Rome 1632, several editions), based on years of research in the catacombs, which appeared posthumously (edited by G. Severano), is still important; the plans and engravings of sarcophagi, inscriptions and especially frescoes are extremely valuable, despite forgeries not known as such at the time. G. Ciampini (1633–1698) produced extensive documentation with ground plans and sketches of churches and engravings of mosaics and paintings; the works *Vetera monimenta* I–II (Rome 1690–1699) and *De sacris aedificiis a Constantino Magno constructis* (Rome 1693) are still very important today; they include pictures of mosaics from Rome and Ravenna which have since been destroyed. F.Buonarotti (1661–1773) with *Osservazioni sopra alcuni frammenti di vasi antichi di vetro ornati di figure trovati ne' cimiteri di Roma* (Florence 1716) and M. A. Boldettti (1663–1749), with *Osservazioni sopra i cimiteri dei santi martiri ed antichi cristiani di Roma*, I–III (Rome 1720), published, among other things, numerous inscriptions and small finds from the catacombs. J. J. Winkelmann (1717–1768), the founder of classical archaeology and the history of Western art, at first had no influence on research into the art of late antiquity and early Christianity; he was concerned with the beauty of ancient art.

The nineteenth century brought a tremendous boom in research and publications which were to be fundamental for all further work. Mention should be made of: C. C. J. Bunsen (1791–1861) with *Die Basiliken des christlichen Roms nach ihrem Zusammenhange mit Idee und Geschichte der Kirchenbaukunst* (Munich 1842), a scientific commentary on the illustrated *Die Basiliken des christlichen Rom. Kupfertafel und Erklärung* (Munich 1822–1827); G. Marchi (1795–1860), who begins *Monumenti delle arti cristiane nella metropolo del cristianesimo* (Rome 1844) with a precise measuring of the catacombs; T. Roller, who in *Les catacombes de Rome* I–II (Paris 1879, 1881) for the first time provides photographs of the catacombs and of numerous sarcophagi. G. B. de Rossi (1822–1894), with *La Roma sotteranea crisitiana* I–II, Rome 1864–1877, and the *Inscriptiones christianae urbis Romae* I–II (Rome 1869–1888) which he began is particularly important; he can be regarded as the founder of 'Christian archaeology' as an independent discipline. See also R. Garrucci (1812–1885), with the monumental *Storia dell'arte cristiana nei primi otto secoli della chiesa* I–VI (Prato 1872– 1880), which published drawings of all the monuments accessible at that time and is thus almost a corpus of early Christian art; F. Piper (1811–1889), who above all with the *Einleitung in die Monumentale Theologie*, Gotha 1880, wanted to emphasize Christian archaeology as a theological discipline; among other things he had the important insight that Christian graphic art did not begin in the apostolic age, but only in the third century CE; E. Le Blant (1818–1897) with *Étude sur les sarcophages chrétiens antiques de la ville d'Arles* (Paris 1878) and *Les sarcophages chrétiens de la Gaule*, Paris 1886. The early Christian sarcophagi in southern France were collected in these works and thus the significance of early Christian Gaul was recognized for the first time.

The nineteenth century already brought an extension of perspective eastwards. Significant material was presented by W. Salzenberg, *Altchristliche Baudenkmale von Konstantinopel* (1857); C. Texier and R. Popplewell Pullan, *L'architecture byzantine*, London 1864; and M.de Vogüé, *Syrie centrale. Architecture civile et religieuse du Ier au VIIe siècle* I–II (Paris 1865–1877). Since the beginning of the twentieth century the whole of the Mediterranean area and neighbouring regions has been investigated, and a great many excavations have been begun. Among researches mention should be made of L. von Sybel with *Christliche Antike* I–II (Marburg 1906–1909); he was a classical archaeologist in Marburg who was the first to work out clearly that early Christian art is completely in the tradition of Graeco-Roman art and is part of it. V. Schultze, *Archäologie der altchristlichen Kunst* (Munich 1895), is a first systematic handbook of early Christian art; he also wrote *Grundriss der christlichen Archäologie* (Munich 1919, Gütersloh 1934) and *Altchristliche Städte und Landschaften*, Leipzig and Gütersloh 1913–1930. J.(= G.) Wilpert produced three monumental corpus-like studies which are still the basis for any work on early Christian art and present the monuments in Rome: *Le pitture delle catacombe romane* (Rome 1903) or *Die Malereien der Katakomben Roms* (Fribourg 1903); *Die römischen Mosaiken und Malereien der kirchlichen Bauten vom 4. bis 13. Jahrhundert* I–IV (Freiburg 1916, part of this has been reprinted with addenda: J. Wilpert and W. N. Schumacher, *Die römischen Mosaiken der kirchlichen Bauten vom 4. bis 13.Jh.* [Freiburg 1976]) and *I sarcofagi cristiani antichi* I–III (Rome 1929–1936). J. Strzygowski in *Kleinasien. Ein Neuland der Kunstgeschichte* (Leipzig 1903) and other works indicated the decisive importance of the East for early Christian art. Finally, F. J. Dölger published studies on 'Antiquity and Christianity'; he also founded the Franz Joseph Dölger Institute for Research into Late Antiquity in Bonn, the *Reallexikon für Antike und Christentum* and the *Jahrbuch für Antike und Christentum*.

Today monuments of the early Christian period have been investigated throughout the former Roman empire and beyond its frontiers, from Spain in the west to Georgia, Armenia, Syria, Iraq,

Jordan and Israel in the east, and from Britain in the north to Algeria, Tunisia, Libya, Egypt, Sudan and Ethiopia in the south. Scholars from numerous countries have been involved.

5. A basic bibliography

In order to get some idea of the appearance of monuments, works with illustrations need to be used; in addition, I have cited some introductions to Christian archaeology and journals and lexicons which are important for early Christian art. See also the catalogues of special exhibitions mentioned in Chapter VII.

Lexicons, journals and proceedings of conferences

Dictionnaire d'Archéologie Chrétienne et de Liturgie 1908–1953 (*DACL*)
Reallexikon für Antike und Christentum Iff., 1950ff. (*RAC*)
Reallexikon zur byzantinischen Kunst Iff., 1966ff. (*RBK*)
Jahrbuch für Antike und Christentum Iff., 1958ff. (*JbAChr*)
Rivista di Archeologia Cristiana 1ff., 1924ff. (*RACr*)
Corso di cultura sull'arte ravennate e bizantina 1ff., 1955ff. (*CR*)
Antiquité Tardive 1ff., 1993ff.
Akten der Internationalen Kongresse für Christliche Archäologie I, 1894ff. (in various languages)
Encyclopedia of the Early Church. Produced by the Institutum Patristicum Augustinianum, ed. A.Di Bernardino I–II, 1992

Introductions, works with illustrations

W. F. Volbach and M. Hirmer, *Frühchristliche Kunst*, 1958
A. Grabar, *Die Kunst der frühen Christentums*, 1969
A. Grabar, *Die Kunst im Zeitalter Justinians*, 1969
C. Andresen, *Einführung in die Christliche Archäologie*, 1971
B. Brenk, *Spätantike und frühes Christentum*, 1977
P. Testini, *Archeologia Cristiana*, ²1980
F. W. Deichmann, *Einführung in die Christliche Archäologie*, 1983
A. Effenberger, *Frühchristliche Kunst und Kultur*, 1988
R. L. Milburn, *Early Christian Art and Architecture*, 1988
H. A. Stützer, *Frühchristliche Kunst in Rom*, 1991
F. Deichmann, *Archeologia Cristiana*, 1993

T. F. Mathews, *The Clash of Gods. A Reinterpretation of Early Christian Art*, 1993

W. Kemp, *Christliche Kunst. Ihre Anfänge. Ihre Strukturen*, 1994

P. C. Finney, *The Invisible God. The Earliest Christians on Art*, 1994

On Coptic art

A. Effenberger, *Koptische Kunst. Ägypten in spätantiker, byzantinischer und frühislamischer Zeit*, 1975

A. Badawy, *Coptic Art and Archaeology. The Art of the Christian Egyptians from the Late Antique to the Middle Ages*, 1978

The Coptic Encyclopedia I–VIII, edited by A. S. Atiya, 1991

II

Architecture

In the early Christian period different kinds of buildings were needed of both a sacred (ecclesiastical) and a profane (secular) kind. These were on the one hand churches, baptisteries and later also monasteries, and on the other hand houses, palaces, market basilicas, baths, reservoirs, fortifications, streets, bridges and so on. Here is a brief description of the most important of these forms of building.

1. Sacred architecture

Christians needed rooms for their cult in which they could hold the common meal (*agape*) and celebrate worship, and also perform baptisms. They also needed somewhere for the instruction of those who wanted to convert to Christianity and be baptized (catechumens); however, nowhere is there any evidence of special rooms for this instruction.

The temples of the Greek and Roman gods were unsuitable for Christian worship. They housed images of the gods; the community gathered in the open air at the altar, on which a priest sacrificed or supervised a sacrifice. By contrast, only the 'initiates', i.e. the baptized, could take part in the climax of Christian worship; it was all a mystery which had to be protected from those who were not called. Other religious communities made similar demands, e.g. in the cult of the deities of Eleusis, of Mithras or of the Egyptian gods, and in Jewish worship. So they chose enclosed premises for their assemblies – as did the Christians.

Graeco-Roman religion did not know a rite comparable to Christian baptism. Thus a special form of building, the baptistery, developed for baptisms. Finally, mention should be made of monastery complexes, which also had no predecessors in the pagan period.

(a) The phases

Thus for their assemblies, for baptisms, instruction and possibly also for interments, Christians needed enclosed areas and structures. Various sources mention these, but there is no archaeological evidence of them for the period before around 200 CE. For instruction, reading from Holy Scripture and the meal, people met in the private house of a member of the community, and baptism could be performed wherever running water was available in some form, in the open air or in a room. *Ecclesia* denotes the Christian community, not the house. The area in which communal cultic actions were performed was merely a secular space, a functional building; it was not hallowed by the cult. All that we know at present indicates that it did not have special architectural features, paintings or reliefs. There may not have been any Christian architecture – or Christian graphic art – before 200 CE. This is suggested by the more general external circumstances, like the situation of small communities in an environment which rejected them or was even hostile to them, and also by the inward attitude of Christians.

This changed around 200 CE: however, so far it has not been possible to establish a more precise chronological point for the change. Later, the edicts under Constantine the Great in 311/313 CE bring a decisive shift. The time in which Christian art slowly begins, between 200 and 311/313 CE, can be called the period before Constantine. Under Constantine the Great the Christian religion could develop freely, and through the initiative of the emperor and his sons numerous churches were founded and richly furnished. So the time of Constantine is an important period for church buildings (311/313–337 or 361). The subsequent years up to 600 CE can be called the period after Constantine.

(i) Before Constantine

In the third century CE the Christian communities grew increasingly large. The first rooms for assemblies will largely have been in private houses. Evidently some of these came into the possession of the community some time during the third century; however, the information in the sources is very imprecise, and there is no archaeological evidence.

Only a very few remains of churches from the time before Constantine have been preserved in the Roman empire; we also know of a small number from various sources, namely inscriptions or

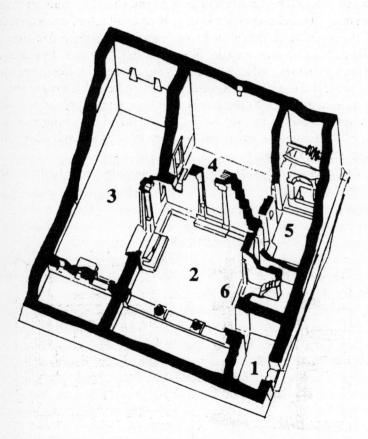

1. Dura Europos, house church (in use between 232/233 and 256; size c.20 x 18 m): 1. entrance; 2. inner courtyard; 3. room for assembly (c.13 x 5 m) with a small podium for the priest's seat on the western narrow side; 4. room for instructing the catechumens (?); 5. baptistery (c.8.90 x 3.40 m; cf. pl.1.1); 6. stairs to the upper storey (where there was perhaps the priest's lodging).

references in literature. In Rome we know the general situation very well. Remains of earlier houses have been found in excavations under numerous churches of the fourth and fifth centuries. Evidently they belonged to fairly well-to-do men or women who put individual rooms or even whole houses at the disposal of the Christian community ('house churches'). The names of the owners were put on small plates at the entrance to the houses (*tituli*); these passed over to the houses and later to the churches built on their location. Such churches are known as title-churches, and eighteen of them can be identified in Rome (e.g. S.Clemente, S.Martino ai Monti, SS.Giovanni e Paolo, S.Sabina). In some cases the remains of ancient houses under the churches are still very impressive sights for present-day visitors, especially those under S.Clemente. However, in none of these sites is it possible to establish precisely which room the community used for the eucharist and the common meal, in which rooms the catechumens were instructed, and where the baptisms took place.

Archaeological evidence of a house church has been found so far

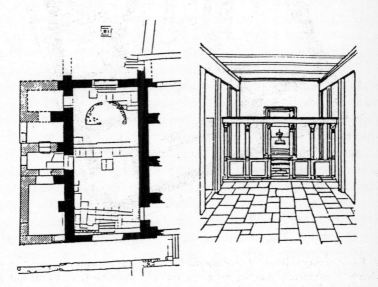

2. Salona (Dalmatia), church (c.300?): ground plan (interior c.16 x 7 m) and sketch of the interior looking west.

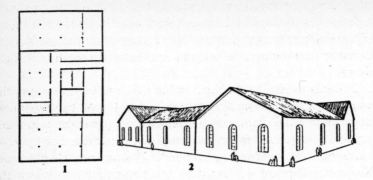

3. Aquileia (Northern Italy), double church (313–319): ground plan (overall dimensions c.38 x 67 m) with north church, linking rooms the use of which is uncertain, and sketch from the south-west.

only in one place in the Roman empire, in the small city of Dura Europos (in eastern Syria, by the Euphrates; diag.1, pl.1.1). A relatively modest private house, separated from the city wall only by a narrow alley, was converted into a church and furnished, probably in 232/233 CE. The city was destroyed by the Sassanids (Persians) in 256 and was not settled in again. So the house served as a church only for two decades. It is the only example that gives us some idea of the rooms in which early Christians gathered and held baptisms, and adds some colour to the scattered and very imprecise written sources, including the Syrian *Didascalia*, a church order from the third century. In the conversion, two smaller rooms were combined into one large one which evidently served as the room where the community met (floor area of around 13 x 5 metres). There is a low podium on the narrow side on which presumably the priest's wooden chair stood. There is no further furnishing, nor did the walls have any decoration. A small room was converted into a baptistery, and scenes from the New Testament and Old Testament were depicted on the walls. The room between the assembly room and the baptistery perhaps served for the instruction of the catechumens. There was an upper storey in the original house; possibly this was kept after the conversion and served as a dwelling for the priest and his family.

There will have been similar modest house churches in numerous other places in the Roman empire. The form of the buildings differed. But in line with Dura Europos, with the least architectural expense private houses may have been converted for the needs of the Christian community. So we can no longer determine all these changes.

Towards the end of the third and in the early fourth century the number of Christians increased considerably. It is probable that now larger church buildings were also erected for particular communities. Only very scant fragments have been preserved. For example Lactantius (*De mortibus persecutorum* XII) mentions a tall church in Nicomedia (present-day Izmit in north-west Turkey) which the emperor Diocletian could see from his palace; during the persecution of Christians in 303 he ordered it to be pulled down. There are other references to larger representative church buildings before Constantine in Eusebius. Bishop Eugenius of Laodicea (near Konya in Turkey), who died in 332, had a long inscription put on his sarcophagus: in it he boasts of having restored a large church building and refers to details of the architecture. We may infer that it was a basilica preceded by an atrium. If Bishop Eugenius had constructed a new building, that would certainly have been clearly emphasized in his epitaph. The original date for the building of the church renovated by the bishop is unknown, but there are some indications that it was before 311/313. Figurative paintings in churches were forbidden at the Synod of Elvira in Spain, which took place around 306 CE. Here, too, we do not know what the churches and the paintings will have looked like. However, these will certainly not have been such modest structures as that in Dura Europos. There is much to suggest that the bishops had in mind large and richly decorated church buildings in Spain.

A few remains of other churches which may possibly date back to the time before Constantine have been preserved. Mention should be made of S.Crisogono in Rome, a large aisleless hall (28 x 15.5m in area), with the main entrance on a narrow side and an open portico on a long side; a small church in Salona (Dalmatia, diag.2) which has been built into older walls, the context of which is not clear; the cave under the church of Thecla in Meriamlik (southern Turkey), which was perhaps transformed into a three-aisle church in the period before Constantine. A building parts of which have been uncovered under the Octagon of Philippi could also belong in this context. This is a relatively large aisleless hall which has an apse at the east end and a prominent entrance at the west end. A mosaic inscription on the floor mentions Bishop Porphyry, who probably took part in the synod in Serdica (Sofia, Bulgaria) in 342. The mosaic inscription is possibly later than the church building, which is thus perhaps to be dated to the period before 324 CE, i.e. before Constantine conquered the east of the empire.

The double church of Aquileia (Northern Italy), which was built between 313 and 319, may give some idea of what larger church buildings looked like in the time before Constantine (diag.3). It consists of two simple halls which, while of considerable size, have very simple forms. Externally they will hardly have differed from large warehouses. Inside, the floors are richly decorated with mosaics, and perhaps we should also suppose that there were wall paintings. It is not certain whether there were churches in basilica form in the period before Constantine. Certainly *basilicae* are mentioned in the sources, for example in connection with North Africa, but we do not know whether this denotes the type of building that we would now call basilica (cf. b ii below).

A small room in a house in Herculaneum (near Naples), which was covered over in 79 CE by the eruption from Vesuvius, is sometimes regarded as a Christian place of worship. There are markings on the wall above a wooden cupboard which have been filled in to form a cross. But there is much to suggest that this reconstruction is wrong and that the room was not therefore used by Christians. A house church from the first century has recently been conjectured in Capernaum (by Lake Genessaret), but so far the excavations have not been published, so that the conjectures cannot be tested.

(ii) The time of Constantine

The edicts of 311–313, and especially the edict of Milan in 313 CE, allowed the Christian religion and recognized it as being on an equal footing with pagan religions (*religio licita*). Since the emperor had formerly also been responsible for the building of temples – along with other founders – Constantine now saw it as his duty to thank the

God who had helped him to victory against Maxentius at the Milvian Bridge in 312, to do something for his own salvation and reputation and to support the Christian communities by building churches. In addition, however, he also had pagan temples renovated and even built new ones, for example in the new capital of Constantinople.

After 313 large numbers of churches were built in many parts of the empire. Many were imperial foundations; others were built by bishops; in some cases it is certain that the churches were built under Constantine, but we do not know who the patrons were. In some cases it is not certain whether the churches go back to Constantine the Great or his sons and successors Constantine II (337–340), Constans (337–350) and Constantius II (337–361). There is sometimes evidence that they were begun by Constantine the Great but only completed later. So these buildings will be included in this section.

It is no longer possible to discover the architecture of the numerous churches of the time of Constantine which are mentioned in literature, since they have completely disappeared; all that

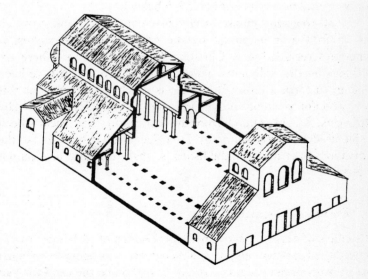

4. Rome, Salvator Church (S.Giovanni in Laterano, begun 313): sketch from the south-east (length c.98 m).

remains of almost all the rest are a few remnants of foundations and small parts of the walls. So as a rule many details of the buildings are uncertain, and they can only be reconstructed in conjectural drawings. The written sources are also important: they are the Papal Chronicle (*Liber Pontificalis*), which in the form extant today goes back to the sixth century but which depicts the time of Constantine very accurately, and two works of Eusebius, the contemporary and supporter of Constantine who was bishop of Caesarea in Palestine (died 339), the *Life of Constantine* and the *Church History*. If we take the archaeological and the literary tradition together, we get a fairly good picture of the churches of the time of Constantine.

It is amazing what a variety of forms can be identified in ground plan and probably also in elevation. The orientation, the number of aisles, proportions, use of arcades or architraves over the columns, the form of the apses and so on differ widely. The first building, the Salvator Church (founded in 313, 'Basilica Constantiniana', now S.Giovanni in Laterano), a foundation of Constantine for the Bishop of Rome, is a five-aisle basilica with an apse at the west end, an entrance at the east end and low additions to the outer aisles in front

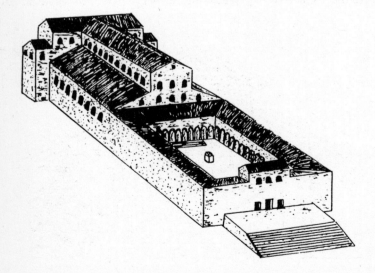

5. Rome, St Peter's (S.Pietro in Vaticano, begun 319): sketch from the south-east (length c.119 m, with atrium c.200 m).

of the apse (diag.4). The church in Tyre (finished in 315) is known only from the sermon given at its inauguration; this indicates that it was a fully developed basilica preceded by an atrium. By contrast, the double structure built in Aquileia in 313–319 under Bishop Theodorus is very modest; both churches will have been halls with wooden supports (diag.3). A much larger five-aisle building is St Peter's in Rome, which was probably begun in 319; one special feature – for the first time in early Christian architecture – is a transept which emphasizes the place of honour, the tomb of the apostle (diags.5–6). The church in El Asnam (Castellum Tingitanum, formerly Orléansville in Algeria), dated by the inscription to 324, also has five aisles but is considerably smaller. The straight east end associates it with later buildings in North Africa. We do not know much about two basilicas in Cirta (Constantine, Algeria), foundations of Constantine. The double church in Trier, begun c.326, is a powerful building: two great basilicas, both with atriums, lie in parallel; the straight east end is unusual. In Rome, Constantine also founded a church dedicated to St Paul on the Via Ostiense, but we do not know what it looked like; it will have been modest and was therefore replaced c.384–400 by a large five-aisle basilica. In

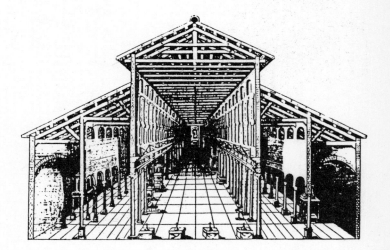

6. Rome, St Peter's: internal view looking east (to the entrance); nineteenth-century engraving (based on a sixteenth-century mural).

S.Croce in Rome (before 324?), an imperial foundation largely reused the walls of the hall of an earlier palace, so the building work was mainly limited to transforming the interior. We have no idea of the nature of churches founded by Constantine in Naples and Capua.

Five churches in Rome are closely connected (diag.7). They lie outside the city walls above cemeteries (SS.Marcellino e Pietro, c.320; S.Lorenzo, c. 326/330; S.Agnese, 338–353; Basilica Apostolorum = S.Sebastiano, founded by Constantine or one of his sons; and an anonymous building on the Via Prenestia, 351–386?). Their special feature is that the aisles run in a U shape round the central nave and form an ambulatory ('ambulatory basilicas', 'cemetery basilicas'). Two are connected with imperial mausoleums, large round buildings (S.Costanza next to S.Agnese, diag 37.2; pl.4; the Tor Pignattara at SS.Marcellino e Pietro; the anonymous building at the Tor dei Schiavi seems to be unconnected with the mausoleum and considerably later); elsewhere, too, there are still

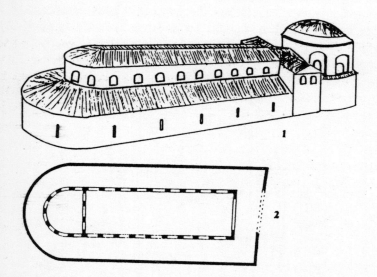

7. Ambulatory basilicas in Rome: 1. SS.Marcellino e Pietro with the tomb shrine 'Tor Pignattara', sketch from the south (c.320; length c.77 m without the shrine); 2. Basilica Apostolorum (S.Sebastiano, time of Constantine, length c.75 m).

tombs in the churches (well preserved in S.Sebastiano). Numerous burials have also been found within several of the churches. So these are covered cemeteries in which memorial meals for the dead were celebrated, and pilgrims could come to the tombs; they were not community churches. Such buildings are not known outside Rome or after the time of Constantine.

After the 'foundation' of Constantinople as the new capital of the empire several churches were endowed there by Constantine. There are no remains of any of them and they are only mentioned, not described more closely, in the sources, so we do not know precisely when the churches were built or what they looked like. Hagia Eirene had a Constantinian predecessor which for a while was extremely important as an episcopal church, but we know nothing of its form. The forerunner of Hagia Sophia, the 'Megale Ekklesia' ('Great Church'), probably goes back to Constantine and – like the subsequent building erected under Theodosius II – may have been a five-aisle basilica, a type of which there is evidence earlier in Rome. Constantine intended the Church of the Apostles as a burial place: it was cruciform (did the arms have one or three aisles?); at the east end a mausoleum (round?) was built for the imperial family. This is the first church of this kind, but later it spread widely. The link between church and mausoleum can also be found in Rome, but in other forms.

After his victory over Licinius in 324 Constantine was sole ruler of the empire. Now he also devoted himself to the places in the Holy

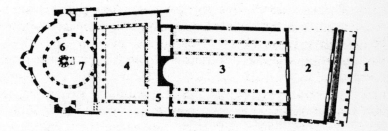

8. Jerusalem, schematic ground-plan of the Church of the Holy Sepulchre (begun 325; overall length c.138 m): 1. entrance from the east; 2. forecourt; 3. five-aisle basilica; 4. courtyard; 5. place of the rock of Golgotha; 6. rotunda over the sepulchre (diameter 33.70 m; cf. pl.1.2); 7. tomb of Christ.

Land, above all after his mother Helena's journey to Palestine in 326. It is also amazing how different the solutions are in these buildings. From 328 on, a tremendous round building with an ambulatory and cupola was built over the tomb of Christ – and thus also the place of his resurrection (Anastasis Rotunda or Sepulchre Rotunda); this was to become the model for a series of early Christian and mediaeval churches (diag.8; pl.1,2). There was a forecourt at the east end and then came a great five-aisle basilica with an atrium. So there is a brilliant link between a centralized martyr-shrine (over the tomb) and a community church in the form of a basilica. St Peter's in Rome is to a certain extent similar, but the development is different (pl.5). A holy place, the Cave of the Nativity, was also emphasized in the Church of the Nativity in Bethlehem, which will have been completed in 333; the church was built for the community and for pilgrims (diag.9). An octagon was built over the cave, and a five-aisle basilica with an atrium was attached on the west side. Another form of building was chosen for the church on the Mount of Olives (Eleona Church), which was also built in 333. This is a simple three-aisle basilica with an atrium in which the holy place, also a cave (in which according to tradition Jesus taught his disciples), lies under the space where the altar is. It should be emphasized that the apse is externally a polygon, a form which recurs later in many churches in the east of the empire. Constantine also built a church at the terebinth and well in Mamre, south of Bethlehem, where Abraham is said to have entertained the deity in the form of three men; this will have been built in 333. It was

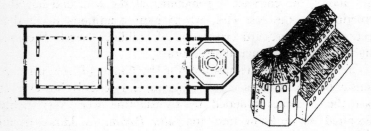

9. Bethlehem, Church of the Nativity (largely finished 333): octagon over the Cave of the Nativity, with an opening in the roof. Ground plan and sketch from the north-east (length c.47 m, with atrium 79 m).

adapted to earlier buildings, very short but broad; it had ancillary rooms at the east end; walls there concealed the apse. These particular features also to some degree anticipate later churches in the Near East.

The cathedral of Antioch on the Orontes, the cultural centre in the Near East, which was begun under Constantine, had quite a different form. It has disappeared, and we do not even know precisely where it stood, but we are to infer from the descriptions that it was an octagon with a prominent apse at the west end; there was a double ambulatory, so the church had five aisles. This is the earliest octagon, and therefore the earliest centralized building with an ambulatory. a form of building which at a later time occurs in a series of examples and many variations (cf. b iii below). Constantine had another church built in Heliopolis (Baalbek, in Lebanon); however, the remains of a basilica with three aisles and three apses at the west end, set within rectangles, do not seem to belong to the Constantinian building, so its form is unknown.

Along with the Salvator Church (S.Giovanni in Laterano), Constantine also endowed a baptistery, S.Giovanni in Fonte (432–440 and greatly altered in the sixteenth and seventeen centuries, pl.18). It was probably round, but was later transformed into an octagon with an ambulatory and an elevated centre with a cupola; the form is in the tradition of rooms in Roman baths and mausoleums. The fact that later baptisteries were predominantly independent buildings with a centralized form goes back to the Lateran baptistery (see iii below).

The churches have an east-west orientation where the lie of the land allows; the entrance is sometimes at the west end but also sometimes at the east end, where local conditions make that necessary. An eastward orientation of buildings largely becomes established after the later fourth century.

The external architecture of the buildings of the time of Constantine seems to have been very simple. Internally, however, at least the churches founded by Constantine were very richly decorated, as we know from the *Liber Pontificalis*, However, no remains have been preserved. Still, the churches of a later time give us some idea of how we might imagine the Constantinian rooms with costly floors, wall coverings, ceilings and so on.

To sum up; within the relatively short duration of the time of Constantine the churches show a great variety of forms, and some have pioneering solutions: the basilica comes into being with different variations, including a transept; the centralized building is used for churches, comprising a round building with an ambulatory, an octagon with ambulatory, and an open cross; finally, the first baptisteries are erected. It is hard to explain why the basilicas immediately display local features in individual countries. Perhaps this is an indication that already before Constantine – e.g. in North Africa and in Syria and Palestine – there had been churches in the form of basilicas, so that the master-builders of the time of Constantine could take up earlier forms.

(iii) After Constantine

In the course of the second half of the fourth century, numerous churches were built not only in the cities but increasingly also in the country. The basilica became established. It underwent a certain standardization, though it took different forms in particular areas. Hundreds of buildings have come down to us, mostly only in the footings and small parts of the rising walls (b ii). In addition centralized buildings are widespread, some with a great wealth of forms, though there are far fewer of them (b iii). Many regions of the Mediterranean display their own special features (e below). Frequently new churches were not built, but older buildings from the time of the Roman empire were reused (c below). Numerous furnishings for churches have been discovered (d below). Monasteries were built (f below) and pilgrimage sanctuaries came into being (g below).

(b) The form of churches and baptisteries: general comments

The churches of the early period have different types of structures. We can distinguish (i) aisleless buildings; (ii) basilicas; (iii) centralized buildings; (iv) square buildings. Finally we shall consider (v) baptisteries, which have various forms.

(i) Aisleless buildings. These are the simplest form for a church and were certainly very common. Many are small and consist of simple

material, others were quite large and were built of squared stones carefully cut. As a rule they had a wooden roof frame, in some areas barrel vaulting, sometimes with wall arches. Sometimes at the east end side rooms were built on the north and south sides resulting in a T form; a tower could be built over the 'crossing'.

(ii) Basilicas. The name comes from the Greek *basilike stoa* ('royal hall') and similar expressions and the Latin derivative *basilica*, which denoted rectangular halls, usually with several aisles. The early Christians adopted the term *basilica* for their churches, but it could also be used to denote buildings with other ground plans, like the aisleless church with the mosaic inscription of Bishop Porphyry in Philippi, S.Stefano Rotondo in Rome (round building, pl.5), or S.Vitale in Ravenna (octagon).

So in the early Christian and Byzantine period *basilica* denoted a church generally. Today art historians understand by basilica a church building with the following properties (diag.10; pls.2–3):
– it must be longitudinal;
– it must have several aisles – at least three;
– the nave must be raised, with a clerestory, an area with windows.
– the main entrance must be at one narrow end and the sanctuary at the other.

The first basilica we can study is the Salvator Church, which Constantine the Great founded in 313 CE for the Bishop of Rome (present-day S.Giovanni in Laterano, pl.4). It is questionable whether there were already basilicas in the time before Constantine. Afterwards basilicas made a triumphal progress all over the Mediterranean and were by far the most widespread form of church; there were numerous local variants. In the early sixth century there was a new development in the Eastern Empire. The longitudinal basilica was fused with the centralized building surmounted with a cupola, and the 'cupola basilica' suppressed the wooden–roofed basilicas as a more elaborate form of building. However, basilicas with wooden roofs continued to be built. In the West the basilica remained the predominant form of building through the early Middle Ages up to the Middle Ages and beyond. The basilica type has various advantages: the buildings are relatively simple to

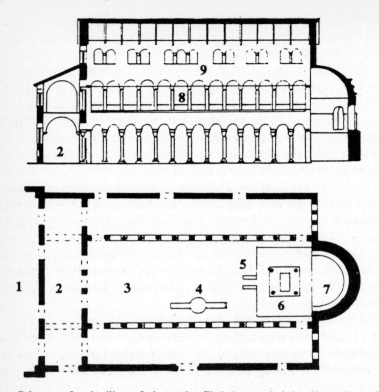

10. Scheme of a basilica of the early Christian period in the region of Constantinople, cross-section and ground plan: 1. atrium (in so far as it exists); 2. narthex (anteroom); 3. naos (nave); 4. site of the ambo ('pulpit'); 5. templon (barrier before sanctuary); 6. site of the altar with ciborium; 7. apse with bench for priests (synthronon); 8. balcony; 9. clerestory.

construct; there are no complicated calculations to make which require highly-qualified professionals; and the forms can be varied in a number of ways.

There is a good deal of discussion about which earlier forms of buildings are the forerunners of the Christian basilica and so what these basilicas derive from. L. B. Alberti (died 1472) already took up this question. We might sum up the discussion by saying that all the individual forms already occur in the Roman architecture of the imperial period, though some of them are very rare. These various elements have been brought together in a novel way on a large scale for Christian basilicas. Perhaps an imperial architectural office was entrusted with the task of erecting a church for the first time in the form of a basilica.

To simplify somewhat, it can be said that the basilicas in the West of the empire are usually longitudinal and have no balconies (pls.2–3); by contrast, within the sphere of influence of the capital, Constantinople, they are often shorter and broader and have balconies (diag.10). However, there are also very long basilicas in the East, though these can usually be explained as special cases (e.g. the pilgrimage church in Lechaion/Corinth).

As a rule the basilicas have three aisles: more elaborate ones have five (e.g. St Peter's, St Paul and the Salvator Church in Rome; Basilica Ursiana in Ravenna; Hagios Demetrios and the basilica under Hagia Sophia in Thessaloniki; the Church of the Sepulchre in Jerusalem and the Church of the Nativity in Bethlehem); by way of exception, some buildings in western North Africa have seven or even nine aisles (e.g. in Carthage). The parts of the basilica are listed in d below.

Usually the basilicas had a wooden roof (diags.6, 21.1; pls.2.2, 3.2), and in some regions barrel-vaulting. Possibly three-aisle buildings were also erected in which the central nave had no clerestory and was not elevated, i.e. 'hall churches'; however they are not confirmed in buildings which have survived, though they can be conjectured (e.g. the double church in Aquileia, diag.3).

There were numerous special forms of basilica. The most important were as follows:

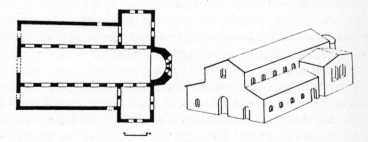

11. Basilica with transept which extends above the level of the aisles (Buthrotum-Butrint, Albania, early sixth century): ground-plan and sketch from the south-west (length c.31 m); cf. pl.6.

1. *With transept.* Beginning with St Peter's in Rome (diag.5), a foundation by Constantine the Great (probably in 319), many basilicas have a crossing before the apse, the transept; often, but not always, this is elevated above the alignment of the side aisles (diag.11; pl.6); in St Peter's it serves to emphasize the venerable tomb, but in most other churches no liturgical or functional reasons can be adduced (there are examples in many areas).

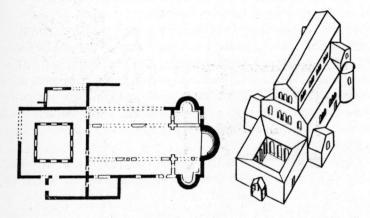

12. Basilica with triconch end and atrium (Durres-Arapaj, Albania, early sixth century): ground plan and sketch from the south-west (length c.65 m).

2. *With a three-conch east end.* In some basilicas there are also conches on the north and south sides as well as the apse (diag.12); this form seems to be a local peculiarity in Egypt and in western Greece, but can also occasionally be found elsewhere (e.g. Hagios Titos in Gortyn; Karabel in Lycia).

3. *With ambulatory.* In a number of basilicas in Rome, including some founded by Constantine, all outside the walls and connected with mausoleums, the side-aisles run round one side in a kind of ambulatory (diag.7); these buildings probably served above all as burial places and rooms for meals in memory of the dead (e.g. S.Sebastiano; S.Agnese); only a very few churches outside Rome have a similar form, and none is precisely the same.

4. *With a towerlike elevation.* Some basilicas had a tower-like

elevation in front of the apse and over a considerable part of the nave and are forerunners of the cupola basilicas (e.g. Lechaion, Alahan Monastir, the 'Zeno Church' in Meriamlik); this expresses the tendency often to be recognized in the Eastern empire to centralize the buildings; the tower was covered with a wooden roof in the form of a pyramid (diag.13; pl.7.1).

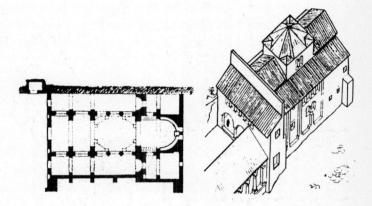

13. Basilica with tower-like elevation above the central nave (Alahan Monastir, southern Turkey, c.500): ground plan and sketch from the south-west (length c.24 m); cf. pl.7.1.

5. *With cupola.* The earliest basilica with a walled cupola (cupola basilica) that we know is Hagios Polyeuktos in Constantinople (524–527; only remnants of the foundations have survived); later, in the reign of Justinian (527–565), numerous further cupola basilicas were built with a wide range of variations; the most famous is Hagia Sophia in Constantinople (532–37).

6. *Other special forms.* Quite a number of basilicas have special features and cannot be fitted into schemes; these include the Church of the Nativity in Bethlehem (begun c.330, diag.9), in which an octagonal central space has been built above the Grotto of the Nativity on to a five-aisle basilica; the cathedral in Trier, in which a powerful rectangular central building rises at the east end of the basilica (begun c.330, centralized building perhaps c.380); and the

Church of the Sepulchre in Corycus (Cilicia, southern Turkey), in which there is a small rectangular space at the east end and cruciform arms lead from it.

(iii) Centralized buildings. Already among the foundations of Constantine there are centralized buildings like the cruciform Church of the Apostles in Constantinople, the 'Golden Octagon' in Antioch and the Rotunda of the Church of the Holy Sepulchre in Jerusalem. Many more were built later. There are forerunners of some of the forms in imperial pagan buildings. The range of variations in the churches is surprisingly large. No type developed among the central buildings which was so widespread and so numerous as the basilica. The most important forms are:

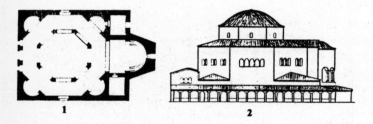

14. Octagons with ambulatory: 1. ground plan of the St George Church in Ezra, southern Syria (date 515, length c.28 m); 2. sketch of the Octagon in Philippi, northern Greece, from the south (sixth-century phase: length c.36.50 m).

1. *Octagon.* The earliest known church is the 'Golden Octagon' which Constantine the Great built in Antioch; it is known only from descriptions and evidently had a double ambulatory – in other words it had five aisles. It had a wooden cupola which was sheathed on the outside with gilded (bronze?) panels.

  (a) *Simple octagon,* sometimes with a cross through it: Binbir Kilisse (sixth century); Nyssa (late 4 century: lost).

  (b) *With ambulatory.* 'Golden Octagon' in Antioch; St Mary's Church on Garizim (484 CE); Octagon of Philippi (first phase, second half of fifth century, diag.14.2); so-called Martyrium of

Philip in Hierapolis (second half of fifth century); St George's
Church in Ezra, south Syria (515, diag.14.1). The Dome of the
Rock, an Umayyad mosque (begun 691/692), gives a good idea of
this.

2. *Three- or four-conch buildings (triconches, tetraconches)*

(a) *Simple tri- or tetraconches*: Triconch in Butrint (probably sixth
century, church?); different buildings in Dalmatia and Greece;
frequently as tomb shrines.

(b) *With ambulatory* (widespread in the Roman empire but not
very numerous geographically: S.Lorenzo in Milan (c.380); triconch
in the library of Hadrian in Athens (early fifth century: diag.15);
Seleuceia in Antioch (c.500; diag.17.1); Bosra (in an external
rectangle, 512/513); Ohrid, Lin and Apameia (sixth century).

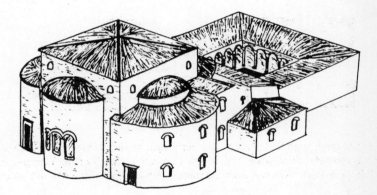

15. Tetraconch with ambulatory: sketch of the building in the Library of
Hadrian in Athens, from the north-east (fifth century at the latest; length
c.66.50 m).

3. *Round buildings*

(a) *Simple circle* (rare). Episkope in Kissamos/Crete (fifth century?); St John's Church in Gerasa (inscribed in a rectangle, 529–
33).

(b) *With ambulatory*: Rotunda of the Church of the Sepulchre in
Jerusalem, founded by Constantine (diag.8; pl.1.2); Hagios Karpos
and Papylos in Constantinople (c.400); S.Stefano Rotondo in Rome

(468–483; diag.5); Apameia (fifth/sixth century); Bosra, 'new
cathedral' (in an external square, early sixth century?).

4. *Open cross.* The first building is probably the Church of the
Apostles which Constantinople the Great had built in Constantinople; its precise form is unknown.

(a) *Cruciform, aisleless.* Hagios Babylas in Antioch (c.380);
Church of the Apostles, now S.Nazaro, in Milan (begun 382);
S.Croce in Ravenna (c.430; destroyed).

16. Cruciform building with multi-aisled arms: sketch of the St John Church in
Ephesus from the south-west (fifth-century phase, length c.116 m).

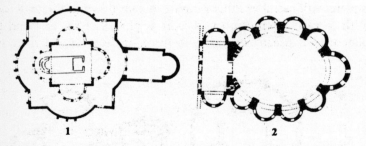

17. Centralized buildings: 1. tetraconch with ambulatory in Seleucia (near
Antioch, early sixth century, length c.55 m); 2. oval building with niches,
Cologne, St Gereon (fourth century at the latest, length c.47 m).

(b) *Cruciform, multi-aisled.* Church of St John in Ephesus (c.450;
diag.16); Church of the Prophets, Apostles and Martyrs in Gerasa

(rectangular walls on the outside, c.465); Qalat Siman (c.480/90, pl. 9.1 and cover picture); churches in Thasos and Salona (second half of fifth century).

5. *Cross inscribed in square/rectangle.* The four arms have barrel vaulting and there is a cupola over the crossing; the corner rooms have different roofs. This type is already attested for smaller churches in the early Christian period (Hosios David in Thessaloniki), but it was predominantly used for baptisteries and other ancillary buildings (e.g. the Al-Mundir building in Resafa, middle of the sixth century; Akkale, c.500; baptistery in Kraneion near Corinth, c.500); from the eighth century this form of building became established for churches and in the middle Byzantine period the 'cross cupola' church was the most widespread type.

6. *Other forms.* Individual churches have other forms; these include St Gereon in Cologne, an oval building with niches in the outside walls (late fourth century; diag.17.2); 'La Daurade' in Toulouse, formally a decagon (c.500?); a hexagonal church in Amphipolis (c.500); or a tetradecagonal building in Binbir Kilisse (sixth century?).

(iv) Square buildings. In northern Mesopotamia (Tur Abdin, southeastern Turkey) a small group of churches has survived, some of them built in a splendid square-cut stone technique; the naves are square with barrel vaulting running in a north-south direction (late fifth or early sixth century: diag.25.2; pl.8.1); at the east end the sanctuary is usually divided into three; at the west end there is a

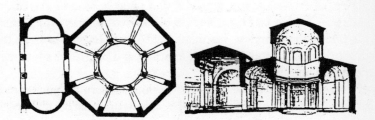

18. Baptistery (S.Giovanni in Fonte) of the Salvator Church (S.Giovanni in Laterano) in Rome (Constantinian foundation, 432–440 and later rebuilt): ground plan and cross-section (through dimension c.18.80 m).

narthex (also with barrel vaulting). The form was probably taken over from pagan oriental temples.

(v) Baptisteries (rooms for baptism). Originally baptism, which marked the acceptance of believers into the Christian community, could take place anywhere that running water could be provided. From the third century on there were also special rooms for baptisms. The baptisms were performed in groups, and up to the sixth century on adults, so the rooms had to be of a certain minimum size.

Centralized buildings were preferred; these were in the tradition of rooms in Roman baths and mausoleums, and often were given a cupola (diag.18). No fixed typology developed, and the range of variations is correspondingly great: octagon (sometimes with conches within it), four and three conches, round (sometimes with ambulatories, and exceptionally with a double ambulatory, pl.10.1), square, cruciform; there were also long rectangular rooms and many special cases.

The piscina (baptismal font) was let into the floor, in centralized buildings usually in the middle. Frequently it is cruciform and has steps at the west end and the east end; however, quatrefoils and other forms also occur.

The earliest extant baptistery is in Dura Europos (c.232/233 CE; diag.1; pl.1.1). The building which Constantine the Great founded along with the Salvator Church (present-day S.Giovanni in Fonte; begun after 313, 423–440 and later changed, pl.18) may have determined the type. Baptisteries since then have been independent buildings, free-standing or attached to a church. One of the early extant ones is that of Hagia Sophia in Constantinople, which was built under the emperor Justinian (532/537). In the later sixth century there was a move to infant baptism, and baptisteries became superfluous buildings.

Evidently in the early Christian period baptism at pilgrimage sanctuaries was especially popular. So particularly elaborate baptisteries are to be found at them (e.g. Qalat Siman, Abu Mina, Tebessa, Alahan Monastir, Lechaion).

In the Middle Ages the early Christian form of the free-standing baptistery constructed as a centralized building was taken up again in different Italian cities, as is shown by the splendid examples in Florence (begun c.1060), Pisa (begun 1152), or Parma (begun 1196).

(c) The conversion of ancient buildings

A large number of earlier buildings in the early Christian period were reused and converted into churches by more or less extensive building operations. There are examples in almost all areas of the Roman empire. Only in rare cases is it possible to determine when the building came to be used for Christian worship, since only exceptionally have new decorations which could indicate this been preserved, and other sources are extremely rare. The earliest examples are the house churches: in Dura Europos we get a good impression of the conversion of a modest private house (in 232/233 CE). The first monumental church is S.Croce in Rome, a foundation of Constantine the Great: parts of an older palace have been used in it for the outside walls, resulting in an unusual ground plan and elevation. The emperor evidently had no inhibitions about the widespread reuse of earlier walls in this instance.

Often temples of the Greek or Roman period were converted into churches. As a rule this was possible only after the edicts of Theodosius (391/392 CE) and above all of Theodosius II (415, 428 etc.). If there are indications, there is much to suggest that the conversions were only made in the second half of the fifth century or even later. One of the latest examples is the Pantheon in Rome, which was consecrated as a church of St Mary in 609.

The conversions took place in different ways. Sometimes the walls of the cella – in so far as they were still standing – and the columns which ran round outside were kept and an apse was simply inserted; or the cella was extended to form a sanctuary. Often columns were erected inside, giving rise to a basilica-like division. Several temples in Athens (the Parthenon, Erechtheion, Hephaisteion, Temple of Ilissos), the temple of Augustus in Ankara and the temple of the Egyptian gods in Pergamon are examples of this. In other cases the external columns were closed in, thus forming the outer walls of the church; the walls of the cella were broken with arcades (e.g. the so-called Concordia temple in Agrigento, the

temple of Athena in Syracuse) or were completely removed and
replaced with columns (e.g. the temple of Zeus in Diocaesarea,
Turkey), producing three aisles. The measures taken in the temple
of Aphrodite in Aphrodisias (Turkey) were very elaborate. The cella
walls were removed and new walls erected outside, around the
temple. Some of the original columns were left standing, but
sometimes they were moved; they now served to separate the aisles.
In addition, an apse was inserted and an atrium put in front of it.
Sometimes a temple was completely demolished and a church built
elsewhere with the material (e.g. the church in the Corycian Cave,
Turkey). Finally, reference should be made to the church complex
in Qanawat (in southern Syria) in which an earlier temple and a large
three-aisle structure with atrium was reused, but the orientation was
completely changed.

Sometimes ancient round buildings were converted into
churches. The most famous example is the Pantheon in Rome. The
measures taken can be seen particularly well in Hagios Georgios in
Thessaloniki. The large round building which had been erected
under Emperor Galerius c.300 CE as a free copy of the Pantheon –
perhaps as a temple to Zeus – was turned into a church in 500; to do
this, an ambulatory with a low penthouse roof was put round it and
the niches were broken through as entrances; at the east end a large
sanctuary with apse was added. The opening in the cupola was
closed and the interior was decorated with splendid mosaics and
marble panels.

Examples of the conversion of different kinds of buildings are:
S.Pudenziana in Rome, which uses parts of a Roman bath; the
Church of St Mary in Ephesus, for which large parts of an unusually
long building from the time of the empire were used; the basilica
which in the late fifth century CE was built into the 'workshop of
Pheidias' in Olympia (from the second half of the fifth century BCE);
a large hexagonal reception room of a palace in Constantinople
which was vaulted and had prominent niches on five sides, and
which in the sixth century was converted into the church of St
Euphemia; the church in Boppard on the Rhine which reuses parts
of the baths of the Roman fortress (late fifth century). A very
elaborate and impressive example is the church which was built into
the north baths of Hierapolis – perhaps in the sixth century (diag.19;

pl.7.2); the original walls were strongly reinforced inwards so that the span of the 'nave' was reduced; the three great compartments were probably roofed with cupolas; an apse was inserted on the south side.

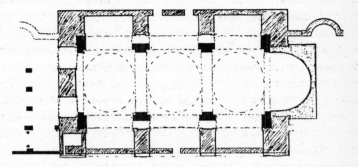

19. Large hall in the north baths of Hierapolis (Turkey), probably second century, converted into a church in the sixth century (?): the black markings indicate the reinforcements which were introduced and the pointed apse to the south; length c.50 m; width c.30 m; cf. pl.7.2.

The churches created by the conversions of ancient buildings have very different ground plans and elevations. The solutions for the upper parts and the roofs were inevitably very varied. In changing the function the idea that the pagan gods had been overcome by Christianity and thus the triumph of Christianity had been documented may have played a part. Often, however, practical considerations may have been dominant; parts of the building which were already standing did not need to be rebuilt and therefore cost nothing; it was considerably cheaper to reuse an ancient building than to erect a new church.

One example of a modern conversion is the 'basilica' in Trier; in the early fourth century it was erected as the throne room of the imperial palace and in 1856 it was restored as a Protestant church.

(d) The parts of the basilica – the furnishing of churches

The basilicas – and similarly churches built in other forms – consist of various parts, not all of which need always be featured. Here the most important will be mentioned; regional peculiarities cannot be taken into account (diags.10,20):

Peribolos: outer wall which divides the sacred precinct from its profane surroundings.

Propylon: prominent doorway which leads into the atrium, the narthex or the church.

Atrium: usually a rectangular forecourt (quadrangle), surrounded by colonnades in more elaborate churches (diags.5,12); usually in front of the narrow west end; exceptionally, where the situation required it, at the east end or on the south side.

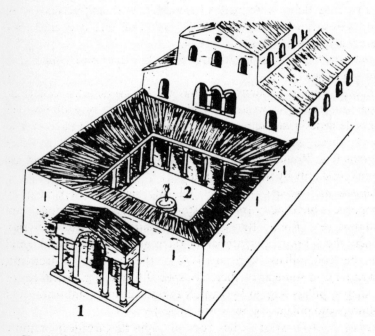

20. Sketch of the atrium of a basilica: 1. propylon; 2. fountain (kantharos).

Krene – phiale – kantharos: fountains in the atrium at which believers washed before entering the church.

Portico: open forecourt of a church, usually on a narrow end (e.g. in Rome, Ravenna), sometimes also on a long side (e.g. in some churches in Syria).

Narthex: enclosed antechamber to the church; frequent, for example, in the Balkans and Asia Minor; in the early Christian period the catechumens (those who had not yet been baptized) had to withdraw to the narthex before the climax of the liturgy, the 'liturgy of the faithful'.

Trivelon: in more elaborate churches an ornate way through from the narthex to the nave, with two columns and three openings, which were closed with curtains (*vela*) before the main part of the liturgy.

Doors: these sometimes have frames with rich decorations and in exceptional cases even bear relief figures (e.g. in Alahan Monastir); as a rule the doors were made of wood (cf. V.2), and perhaps were sometimes covered with sheets of bronze; on rare occasions they were made of massive cast bronze.

Naos: area for the congregation; in a basilica this consists of a nave and side aisles.

Balcony: in more elaborate churches in the East (southern Balkans, Asia Minor) and in western North Africa there are galleries over the side aisles and the narthex which run round the nave in a U shape; these are intended for the women (*gynaikonitis*). In other regions (e.g. Rome, Ravenna, Syria) balconies are unusual and are to be found only by way of exception.

Columns and pillars: the nave and side aisles are separated by supports which bear the clerestory; in many areas these are columns (e.g. Rome, Ravenna, the Balkans, Asia Minor, Syria). Where the appropriate material for them was unavailable and could not be got, pillars were used (e.g. the basilica in Burtrint, diag.21.1). In some areas there are special forms, e.g. cruciform or T-shaped pillars (e.g. in Syria, pl.8.2), and various combinations of columns and pillars (e.g. in North Africa).

Arcades – architraves: arches rest on supports (arcades) or more rarely there are straight 'beams' of stone, usually shaped and ornamented (architraves).

Capitals: columns – and sometimes also piers – bear capitals as a transition to the arcades or the architrave; in the East and e.g. also in Ravenna there are sometimes also supports on the capitals ('transoms', pl.14.1). For the form of capitals see the table of types (diag.22). Corinthian capitals or composite capitals of different

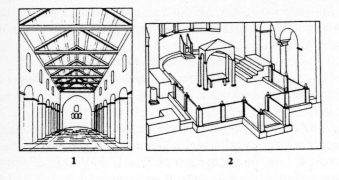

21. Basilicas: 1. internal view of basilica with piers, looking eastwards (Butrint, cf. diag.11; pl.6.2); sketch of a sanctuary with templon (barrier), prominent door in the centre ('royal door'), altar with ciborium, priest's seats at the sides and in the apse, and cathedra for the bishop in the middle.

22. Forms of capital: 1. Corinthian capital; 2. composite capital (with 'denticulated acanthus'); 3. capital with 'windswept' leaves; 4. two-zone capital with animals; 5–7. Ionic transom capitals.

forms are usual (pls.14.1–3), going back to models from the Roman imperial period; two-zone examples with animal figures (pl.15.2) and instances with 'windswept' leaves (pl.15.1) are rarer. In late antiquity the 'Ionic transom capital' came into being, through a fusion of Ionic capitals with transoms (pl.14.4); these were mostly used on balconies and in other subordinate places.

Wall decoration: the walls above the arcades are sometimes covered with panel mosaics; these were followed by wall paintings or mosaics.

Windows: in windows with several divisions, these are separated by capitals which have special shapes and are therefore easy to recognize; they are pillars on which inner and outer half-columns are put (all of a piece); the capitals are stretched.

Roofs: in some churches one could look up into the open roof frame (diags. 6, 21.1); the thick cross beams were possibly carved and painted. Panelled wooden ceilings with painted fields were also widespread. In western North Africa and some other areas clay tiles with relief figures which served as coffers have been found. The barrel-vaulted basilicas and the centralized buildings surmounted with a cupola are special cases.

Floors: these consisted of larger or smaller stone slabs, carefully laid, of tesselated or panel mosaics, and in modest churches of clay tiles or composition (cf.4.4).

Seats for the congregation: sometimes benches have been preserved which were built along the inner walls of the aisle; moreover there were probably wooden seats. However, it was usual to stand during the liturgy.

Bema (from the Greek *bema*, step): sanctuary which only priests and deacons might enter, separated from the nave by screens; usually somewhat higher than the *naos* (diag.21.2).

Apse: at the east end the sanctuary usually had an apse which externally formed a semicircle; it was roofed with a semi-cupola. This had a round (e.g. in Rome, Greece) or polygonal (e.g. in Constantinople, Ravenna) exterior. There are many special forms in the provinces. In eastern parts of the empire small side rooms (sometimes called *parabemata*) can be found north and south of the apse – as an extension of the aisle. In Syria and Palestine reliquaries were put in them and relics were venerated. In Asia Minor and in the southern Balkans, from the sixth century (?) they served as 'pastophoria' (sacristies); in the northern room (*prothesis*) the eucharist was prepared, while liturgical vessels and vestments were kept in the southern room (*diakonikon*).

Various furnishings were in the churches – aisleless halls, basilicas and centralized buildings – which were necessary or desirable for the liturgy:

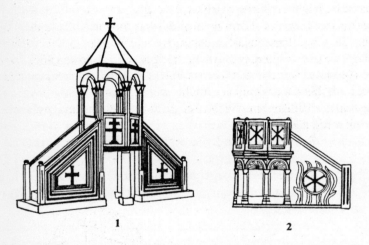

1   2

23. Ambo ('pulpit'): 1. with two flights of stairs and built in the form of a baldachino; 2. With one flight of stairs.

Ambo (from the Greek *anabaino*, 'go up'): a kind of pulpit from which the deacon read the gospel; it stood in the nave, outside the *bema* (sanctuary), often south of the central axis of the church. The forms are very different; sometimes only one flight of stairs leads to the platform (diag.23.2), in more elaborate examples two (diag.23.1; pl.15.3); grandiose examples with special forms are rare.

Solea: a barrier running from the *templon* in the nave to the *ambo*.

Templon: a barrier which separates the nave from the sanctuary (*bema*) (diag.21.2). There is an entry ('royal gate') in the middle which can be richly decorated. The *templon* consists of pillars with panels between them. The pillars are sometimes low with bosses on the top; sometimes they are higher and carry a beam (architrave); they are easy to recognize, as they have hollows in the side in which the panels were let. There were recesses in the floor for piers and panels, at the level of the *bema*; they often make it possible to reconstruct the *templon*, even if there are only a few fragments. The panels (Greek *thorakia*, Latin *cancelli*) are usually rectangular and have different forms of decoration, ornamental (pl.13.1), with vegetation and rarely also figured motifs (pl.13.2); very elaborate pieces are made in filigree marble (pl.13.3).

Altar (Greek *trapeza*, Latin *mensa*): this has the form of a table with four or more legs (usually columns) which bear a flat surface (diag.24.2); often there is a slab on the floor with hollows which took the columns. Sometimes there is a further rather larger rectangular recess on this slab; a reliquary might have stood in it.

Ciborium: a baldachino which rests on four columns and rises over the altar (diag.24.2).

24. Furnishings for early Christian churches: 1. cathedra; 2. ciborium with altar (mensa, trapeza).

Synthronon: seats for the priests, usually in a semicircle round the apse, with a variable number of steps leading up to them.

Cathedra: throne for the bishop in the centre of the *synthronon*, made of wood, stone (diag 24.1) or – in one extant exception (Maximian's cathedra, Ravenna) – ivory.

Tables: sometimes there were one or more other tables in the churches on which the faithful put gifts intended for the poor; the table tops sometimes have borders decorated with reliefs.

In very simple churches some of the furnishings will have been made from wood. If the church had rather more resources, stone from the neighbourhood, limestone or local marble, was used. It was a particularly widespread custom to take columns and capitals from earlier buildings which had been abandoned, mostly from the time of the Roman empire, and to use them as 'spoils'. Thus in Rome, for example, so many columns and capitals were available that hardly any new decoration had to be made for the early Christian churches.

In more elaborate churches in other areas (e.g. Ravenna, the Balkans, Asia Minor, North Africa, Abu Mina in Egypt), people were often very extravagant and imported the columns, capitals, ambo, templon with side panels and perhaps even the altar and ciborium. On the island of Proconnesus (Marmara) in the Propontis (Sea of Marmara) near Constantinople (Istanbul), a series of such pieces were made which were coveted in wide areas of the Mediterranean. They are mostly recognizable first by their style but secondly by the material used: the marble from Proconnesus is relatively coarse-grained, light grey, and has dark, irregular stripes. A ship which sank at Marzameni (near Syracuse) was evidently laden with furniture for just one church and came from Proconnesus. We do not know its destination: it could have been a place in Italy, but perhaps also in the Balkans. The load comprised twenty-eight sets of columns, capitals and beams, twelve screen panels with small pillars and columns, the altar and four supports for the ciborium, all made of marble from Proconnesus; by contrast the ambo was made of green speckled marble (*verde antico*) which came from Thessaly; the original weight of all these pieces was 76–77 tonnes.

The manufacturers on Proconessus spread the style of Constantinople for capitals, plates, ambos and so on; this was regarded as the model and was often imitated in the provinces, e.g. in limestone or local marble. Columns of cipollino ('little onion') marble from the quarries at Carystus in the south of the island of Euboea were also greatly coveted, and various pieces of furniture from the marble with coarse green speckles (*verde antico*).

(e) Forms of church buildings in the provinces of the empire

Very few remnants of churches from the time before Constantine have survived, and we know of others only from written sources. No local differences can be recognized in the forms.

The amazing thing about the churches of the time of Constantine is their variety of form. Buildings in Rome, North Africa (El Asnam) and the Near East (Jerusalem, Bethlehem, Mamre, Antioch) show some special features which can also be found in later churches of these areas. So evidently local styles of building had already developed in the time of Constantine. However, these differences become clearer in the main group of churches from this period, i.e. from the late fourth to the early seventh century. The buildings of individual areas differ in a series of points: in details of ground-plan and elevation, proportions, the use of balconies, the roofing (wooden roof, stone barrel vaulting, etc.), the form of supports (columns, different kinds of pillars or a combination of columns and pillars), the shape of the apses (rounded, polygonal, open or enclosed), the building technique (bricks, quarried stone, square-cut stone, alternation of materials in layers, etc.), the external shape of the buildings (e.g. with blind niches or decorated all round), the windows, the architectural ornamentation, etc.

The most important architectural areas are listed below with some of their characteristics; further information is given in the bibliography (Ch.VIII below). In the case of special forms, etc., only individual examples are given; not all are listed.

Rome. Basilicas predominate, mostly with three aisles (S.Sabina, diag.2, and S.Maria Maggiore are well preserved); exceptionally there are five aisles (Salvator Church = S.Giovanni in Laterano, diag.4; St Peter's, diags 3–6; St Paul), with architrave or arcades and columns. Sometimes there are transepts (St Peter's, St Paul). The ambulatory basilicas with pillars as supports (S.Sebastiano, diag.7;

S.Agnese, etc.) are special cases in the architecture of the early
Christian period generally. Only one centralized building, a complicated round building with an ambulatory, has survived (S.Stefano
Rotondo, pl.5). The exterior of the churches is simple. The walls are
made of brick. On one narrow end there is an entrance hall (portico),
or more rarely an atrium. As a rule there is a rounded apse (pl.2.1)
and in one exceptional case a polygonal one (S.Giovanni a Porta
Latina). The nave is illuminated by large windows in the clerestory;
the side aisles usually seem to be dark. Internally the walls were
decorated with panel mosaics, tesselated mosaics and wall paintings;
columns and capitals are almost always older pieces (spoils) which
have been reused (spoils) from earlier buildings. Panel mosaics or
large slabs form the floor.

Ravenna. A unique number of well-preserved churches and other
sacred buildings have survived in this city (pl.3); furthermore, some
have been excavated. Ravenna became the imperial residence in 402
and was developed on a grandiose scale; however, in the Middle
Ages and modern times it had no significance, so the old churches
were not replaced or substantially changed. Basilicas with three
aisles predominate, without a transept (S.Giovanni Evangelista;
S.Apollinare Nuovo, pl.3.2; S.Apollinare in Classe, pl.3.1); there is
one 'broad-arcaded basilica' of the kind typical in Syria (S.Michele
in Africisco); a five-aisle basilica with five aisles has not survived
(Basilica Ursiana); there is also an 'open cross' (S.Croce, only parts
of the foundations have survived) and an octagon with an ambulatory
(S.Vitale). The baptisteries of the Orthodox and the Arians, the
Archiepiscopal Chapel, the 'Mausoleum of Galla Placidia'
(diag.37.1; pl.17.1) and the Mausoleum of Theoderic, along with
remnants of Theoderic's palace, supplement the picture. The walls
of the buildings are made of brick and are enlivened outside by blind
arches. At the west end most of the churches usually have a portico,
and rarely an atrium. The apses are often broken (polygonal); in late
churches there are subsidiary rooms (*parabemata*) at the east end.
Large windows are put in the clerestory and the side aisles, which
admit a good deal of light into the church. The columns and capitals
and the transoms (the supports between the capitals and the arches,
pls.13.1; 14.1) are almost all imported from Constantinople, as are
some of the other furnishings. The churches and baptisteries were

decorated with rich mosaics, of which considerable remains have been preserved.

Milan. The city was often an imperial residence after 353 CE, and between 380 and 402 CE it was the preferred residence; in 374 Ambrose (died 397) became bishop, and several churches were erected in his time. Fragments of some have been preserved or can be demonstrated; they have unusually varied forms: three-aisle basilicas, simple (S.Ambrogio) or with a transept (S.Simpliciano); a five-aisle basilica with a cancelled east end (S.Tecla); 'open cross' (S.Nazaro); tetraconch with ambulatory and probably a cupola (S.Lorenzo). Brick was the principal material; the walls were enlivened outside with blind arches (preserved in S.Simpliciano). Sparse remains show that there were costly decorations with tesselated and panel mosaics.

The Balkans, the Aegean islands. A large number of churches have been preserved, and these can be divided into different local groups. They are predominantly basilicas, usually with three and occasionally with five aisles (Thessaloniki, Hagios Demetrios and the basilica under Hagia Sophia; Epidauros); sometimes there are three conches at the east end (western Greece; Durres-Arapaj, diag. 12; Gortyn on Crete, Hagios Titos), sometimes a transept (Nikopolis; Butrint, diag.11; pl.6, Philippi A); exceptions are cruciform basilicas (Salona; Thasos) with a tower over the crossing (Lechaion). The centralized buildings are very varied: simple triconches (Dalmatia, Butrint), tri- and tetraconches with ambulatory (Lin; Ohrid; Athens, building in the library of Hadrian, diag.15), an octagon (Philippi, diag.14.2) and a hexagon (Amphipolis). The material is usually quarried stone, and in very splendid buildings also square-cut stone; sometimes layers of brick are inserted (Thessaloniki). The apses are usually rounded. In areas which were strongly influenced by the capital, Constantinople, the more elaborate churches have balconies. Architectural decoration is often imported from Constantinople (pl.13.3; 14.2); in numerous areas there are indigenous copies, in local marble (pl.13.4) or in limestone. Often floor mosaics have been preserved, but only rarely wall and ceiling mosaics (e.g. Thessaloniki), and only exceptionally fragments of wall paintings (Demetrias; Stobi).

Constantinople. The city became capital of the empire in 324/330 and was endowed with numerous churches. Since it is still largely inhabited, very few have survived; there are written sources for some buildings. There were three-aisle basilicas (St John Studios is the best example), a five-aisle basilica (a predecessor of Hagia Sophia, fifth-century phase), a cruciform church (Holy Apostles, details unknown), a round church (Hagios Karpos and Papyluo, construction unknown) and finally a basilica with cupola (Hagios Polyeuktos, built 524–527). St John Studios is relatively short and wide and has an atrium, a narthex, a polygonal apse and balconies; the walls are made of layers of cut stone and bricks. Such proportions seem typical of Constantinople and its area of influence. The architectural decoration is of high quality and consists of marble from Proconnesus. The capitals and other architectural sculptures of Hagios Polyeuktos are also fine pieces of work. Hardly anything is known of the rest of the decoration of these two churches or of others. Scanty remains of wall mosaics have been found in Hagios Polyeuktos.

Asia Minor. There are several architectural regions which differ in forms of building, material used and mode of construction: the special features in Lycia (south-western Turkey), Cappadocia (south-east of Ankara), Binbir Kilisse (south of Konya) and above all in a large number of buildings in Cilicia (eastern part of the southern coast) are easily recognizable. In addition there are isolated churches, e.g. in Nicaea (Iznik), Ephesus and Miletus. These are mostly three-aisle basilicas, sometimes with balconies; special buildings are a cruciform church (Church of St John in Ephesus,

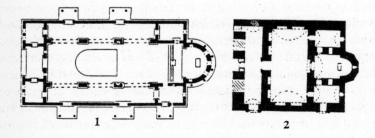

25. Forms of building typical of Syria and Mesopotamia: 1. basilica with broad arcades (Qalb Louzeh, c.500; length c.38 m); 2. square building (Salah, Mar Yakub; c.500, length c.23 m, width 20 m); cf. pl.8.1.

fifth-century phase, diag.16), a triconch ending (Lycia), a vaulted nave (Binbir Kilisse) and tower-like elevations above the centre of the nave (Alahan Monastir, diag.13; pl.7.1, Dag Pazari). Different kinds of centralized buildings are attested above all in Binbir-Kilisse, and a complicated octagon in Hierapolis ('Martyr Shrine of St Philip'). Sometimes, above all near the coast, there is architectural decoration imported from Proconnesus (pl.13.2); often, too, there are local products in marble and above all in limestone. Floor mosaics have been preserved only in a few cases and there are only the tiniest fragments of wall mosaics and paintings.

Syria, northern Mesopotamia. A large number of churches have been preserved which in form, material and mode of construction can be assigned to smaller architectural provinces. Above all the limestone area of north-west Syria, Resafa, the Tur Abdin (northern Mesopotamia, present-day south-east Turkey) and the volcanic Hauran (southern Syria) differ from one another. Three-aisle basilicas with wooden ceilings predominate. The small group of 'broad-arcaded basilicas' (diag.25.1) with rectangular or cruciform pillars and very large arcades are typical of Syria; outside the area we know of only one parallel (Ravenna, S.Michele in Africisco). Qalb Louzeh in the limestone region of northern Syria and basilica A in Resafa (pl.8.2) are particularly impressive. The great cruciform basilica of the pilgrimage sanctuary of Qalat Siman is a special case; the centre forms an octagon which surrounds the pillar on which St Simeon spent some decades in ascetic practices (pl.9). Some of the basilicas of the Hauran have a special form and are roofed with slabs. Among the scattered centralized buildings there are octagons (Antioch, lost; Ezra, St George's Church, pl.14.1), a round building (Apameia) and several tetraconches with ambulatory (Seleucia, diag.17.1; Apameia; Diyarbakir; Bosra). Large aisleless churches and square buildings are characteristic of the Tur Abdin; these are an exception in early Christian architecture generally (diag 25.2; pl.8.1). One characteristic of many churches in Syria is that there are several subsidiary rooms next to the main apse; often reliquaries have been found in them, so the rooms served for the veneration of martyrs. Several baptisteries have been preserved, including the early one in Nisibis (Nusaybin in south-east Turkey) and the significant building in Qalat Siman. Usually the churches are built of squared stone carefully cut (pls.8.1; 9). In north-western Syria limestone has been used; the exterior is sometimes richly decorated, and the capitals and other ornaments, which are local work, are splendid. Good local architectural decoration has also been preserved in Resafa. The basalt in the Hauran is difficult to work, and there are only very simple capitals, etc. Floor mosaics have been preserved in some buildings, but nothing is known of wall paintings or mosaics.

Palestine, Arabia. In these provinces, too, smaller architectural areas can be seen which differ by virtue of the special features of the architectural forms. The churches are usually three-aisle basilicas with wooden roofs; sometimes there are two smaller subsidiary rooms on the north and south sides of the main apse, and often the apses have a rectangular wall round them at the east end. As in Syria, relics were often venerated in the subsidiary room on the south side. There are centralized buildings e.g. in Beth Shean (round with an ambulatory), Gerasa (inscribed cross, round), Gadara (an octagon inside a square) and on Mount Gerizim (Church of St Mary, octagon). The Constantinian Church of the Nativity in Bethlehem and the Church of the Holy Sepulchre in Jerusalem are special cases in early Christian architecture (diag.8; pl.1.2).

The churches are usually built in more or less large, square-cut stones, sometimes irregular. The exterior is simple. Numerous floor mosaics have been preserved. Above all near the coast the decoration consists of pieces imported from Proconnesus; otherwise there is local work in various materials.

Egypt. We know of a series of widely scattered churches; often they have been inserted into older buildings. They are mostly three-aisle basilicas which often have a triconch east end. The capitals and other parts of the decoration are local work. The churches in the pilgrimage sanctuary of Abu Mina are connected with the architecture of the capital city and other areas of the kingdom, and differ from those in the rest of Egypt. The building decoration in Abu Mina also seems predominantly to have been imported.

North Africa. In present-day Libya only a few churches have been investigated, but numerous churches have been excavated in Tunisia and Algeria. These are only basilicas, usually three-aisle and in several cases five-aisle; exceptionally (in Carthage) there are seven and – in one case – nine aisles. Sometimes the nave is elevated by columns; a tower may have been built above it, but it is uncertain how it was roofed. The apses often have a rectangular wall over them. A characteristic of North Africa is the 'counter-apse', a second apse at the west end of the nave; in several cases it has been built later and contains tombs, e.g. of martyrs (there are parallels in Spain). Another peculiarity of the churches in North Africa is that often combinations of columns and pillars are used as supports. Often the walls are made of stone 'chequer work', i.e. larger long blocks with smaller stones inserted. The buildings of the Tebessa group have rich ornamentation; the others are more modest. In some cases there are floor mosaics, but nothing is known about the rest of the decoration.

Spanish peninsula. The very few churches which have been excavated, and of which the remains are scanty, are three-aisle basilicas. A peculiarity of some is that – like buildings in North Africa – they have an apse on both narrow ends (basilicas with counter-apses or double apses); the apse at the west end seems to have served predominantly for burials. Because of the bad state of preservation it is almost impossible to say what the churches looked like. Very little decoration has been found, but often parts of floor mosaics have been preserved.

Gaul, the Rhine-Moselle region. There are very few churches from the early period, so it is not possible to determine the peculiarities of individual districts; special cases are the cathedral in Trier, which consists of a double church (perhaps begun around 330; the eastern part of the north church was developed into a powerful square building around 380); St Gereon in Cologne, an oval with niches (late fourth century, pl.17.2); and 'La Daurade' in Toulouse, now completely lost, which was formerly a decagon (c.500). Several baptisteries have been preserved in southern France, though they have been heavily restored (e.g. Fréjus, Poitiers and Aix-en-Provence); these have different forms. The baptistery of Trier cathedral is also unusual, with a large rectangular piscina; and there is an aisleless church in Boppard with the baptismal font in the interior. Little is known of the architectural decoration. In Gaul there are some pieces imported from Proconnesus and some native work; in Cologne and Trier older capitals sometimes seem to have been reused (Trier, cathedral; Cologne, St Gereon). Floor mosaics are only preserved in exceptional cases (southern France; Cologne, St Gereon). Wall mosaics are only attested in literary evidence (Toulouse, La Daurade; Cologne, St Gereon).

(f) Monasteries

Already in early Christianity, asceticism was thought to be particularly well pleasing to God. There is evidence of itinerant ascetics and anchorites (hermits) at least from around 260. Anchoritism became particularly popular as a result of Antony the Great (251/252). He had withdrawn into the Natron valley (Wadi Natrun), north-west of Cairo, and numerous other anchorites followed him there. Antony is therefore regarded as the 'father' of monasticism. The anchorites lived according to their own ideas and there was no fixed organization. The collection of hermitages in Kellia (similarly north-west of Cairo) is still impressive today. The first were built in the fourth century, but the great heyday came in the sixth and early seventh centuries. A large number of anchorites settled there. Each had his own little walled farmstead with a chapel, totally built of air-dried clay bricks. To the present day, on a surface of about 100 square kilometres, more than 1500 settlements can be registered. Moreover there are several churches in which services could have been held at certain times.

The first monastery was built by Pachomius around 320/325 at Tabenissi, in a loop of the Nile in Upper Egypt. He decreed very strict rules which laid down the communal life of the monks and then also the nuns in detail. This gave rise to the 'coenobitic' form of monasticism. Another eight monasteries and two nunneries were to be founded in Upper Egypt during his lifetime (c.287–342). This indicates a large number of recruits; it is reported that around 1000 monks or nuns lived in each of them. Basil the Great (328/331–379), Bishop of Caesarea in Cappadocia, gave monasticism more moderate forms, and monastic life spread rapidly in the Mediterranean. The first monastery in the capital, Constantinople, was founded in 383. Finally, the fifth and sixth centuries brought a great heyday for the monasteries.

There is so far no archaeological evidence for the first monastery in Tabenissi and the subsequent foundations, so we have no idea how the complexes were organized. Only the remains of buildings from the second half of the fifth and the sixth centuries are known. However, on the whole the tradition is very uneven. There are examples from Egypt, Palestine, Syria, and some remote areas in Asia Minor (Cilicia, Isauria, Lycia), but not from the West of the empire and the Balkans.

26. Monastery complex (north-west monastery in Deir Siman, north-west Syria, c.500): sketch from the north-west (overall length c.80 m).

There do not seem to have been fixed rules for the building of monasteries (diag.26). Some structures are very small and have a solitary location. Monasteries in the wilderness of Judaea might be mentioned as an example. Others were larger complexes with numerous buildings, which are to be seen in some monasteries in northern and southern Syria. Often monasteries developed into places of pilgrimage; this can be traced e.g in Alahan Monastir, which was extended in stages and enlarged with new buildings. On

various occasions monasteries seem to have been 'service organiza-
tions' in pilgrimage centres. Thus alongside the tremendous
cruciform pilgrimage church of Qalat Siman there is a monastery
whose monks may have been responsible for running the whole
place; in Telanissos (Deir Siman), below Qalat Siman, there are
several monasteries, some of which may have looked after the
pilgrims (diag.26).

There were also monasteries within the cities, but virtually no
traces remain. The monastery of St John, which was founded by a
Studios (in 453?) near the land wall of Constantinople, within the
city, deserves special attention. It was of great importance over the
centuries. The church has been preserved as a ruin, but all that is left
of the monastery is a large cistern, so we have no idea of what it
looked like from the outside.

The arrangement of individual buildings in a monastery differs
widely. The church is important. There is no special type for it, so
monastery churches cannot be distinguished from community
churches. Sometimes there is just a nave, but in larger monasteries
there is a three-aisle basilica. In addition there are ancillary
buildings, storerooms and accommodation for monks or nuns and
guests. However, extant remains of buildings can only be defined
more closely in exceptional cases. Thus for example we do not know
what form the cells had or how they were arranged. As a rule living
rooms and ancillary buildings seem to have been built much less well
than the church, so that they have fallen into ruin or are no longer
extant. These buildings are often connected to the church, and
sometimes they are attached to its right-hand corner. On occasion
the buildings and the church are enclosed with a wall to provide a
courtyard. Sometimes there is also a tower to which the inhabitants
of the monastery could retreat in times of danger, or certain monks
could retire for special ascetic practices. In endangered frontier
areas of the kingdom monasteries were walled like small fortresses.
If they were in safe areas, they did not have a surrounding wall (e.g.
Alahan Monastir).

(g) Pilgrimage sanctuaries

Already in the time of Constantine, the tombs of martyrs who were

specially venerated, or holy places, were incorporated into the
churches, emphasized by architectural features and made accessible
to believers. This can be seen in St Peter's in Rome, the Church of
the Holy Sepulchre in Jerusalem, the Church of the Nativity in
Bethlehem or the cathedral in Trier. Pilgrimages to places in the
Holy Land began after 324/325 CE, and boomed considerably after
Helena, the mother of Constantine the Great, undertook a pilgrimage in 326. Pilgrim literature begins with the Pilgrim of Bordeaux,
who travelled to the Holy Land in summer and autumn 333 and
composed a report.

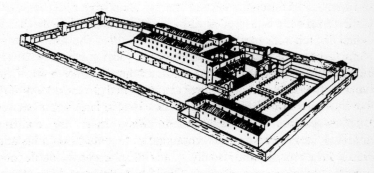

27. Pilgrimage place (Tebessa-Theveste, Algeria, c.500): sketch from the
north-west (area of the whole precinct c.190 x 90 m).

In the later fourth century and above all in the fifth century,
church buildings were erected for many martyrs and saints. Some
attracted numerous pilgrims, so that extensive building measures
were necessary to cope with the crowds. Often this had an effect on
the form of the churches, which display unusual and individual
features. Moreover further buildings had to be erected to serve the
needs of the pilgrims. There was no scheme for the overall
arrangement, so each place of pilgrimage had its own character.
Particularly striking examples are Qalat Siman (in the limestone area
of north-western Syria) between 475 and 491 CE, built on the place
where the monk Simeon (386–459) had spent many years in ascetic
practices on a pillar (pl.9); Meriamlik (Ayatekla, near Seleucia ad
Calycadnum, present-day Silifke, in southern Turkey), where a cave

was connected with the last retreat of Thecla, an alleged disciple of
Paul; the extension with a number of churches, etc,. began around
375 CE; Abu Mina ('Menas town', near Alexandria in Egypt) with
the tomb of St Menas, who is said to have suffered martyrdom in 296
(the extension with a number of churches took place above all in the
fifth and sixth centuries); Tebessa (Theveste, eastern Algeria,
diag.27), around 500 CE, probably erected over earlier buildings,
perhaps in honour of St Crispian, who is said to have suffered
martyrdom during Diocletian's persecution of Christians in 305 CE
and who was one of the principal saints of Africa; Lechaion (near
Corinth), with an extraordinarily large basilica, after 450 CE,
perhaps built in honour of the martyr Leonidas and the seven
women who were martyred with him; Hagios Demetrios in Thessaloniki, which was erected in the second half of the fifth century
over earlier predecessors, in honour of the warrior saint Demetrios
and restored in the seventh century after an earthquake, a powerful
five-aisle basilica with a prominent transept, located in the city.

While each of these arrangements is quite different, some
common features can be established. The churches are relatively
large and are erected on sub-structures, so that they could be seen
from a long way off, and usually stand out in a prominent place of
honour. As the remains show, they had splendid decoration.
Sometimes there are several churches in one complex. It seems to
have been a particularly popular practice to be baptized at pilgrimage
sanctuaries. So there are usually baptisteries, sometimes of a
considerable size, which were designed for the baptism of numerous
people. Often there are streets and squares which served for
processions and other ceremonies. There were lodgings for prominent pilgrims in or near places of pilgrimage. Water had to be
brought in and possibly stored in cisterns. Baths served the pilgrims
and also the clergy. Monks – and perhaps also nuns? – looked after
these facilities and cared for the pilgrims, and possibly also regulated
the course of ceremonies. They also produced and sold devotional
materials. There needed to be accommodation for monks and nuns
and perhaps also a separate church. The priests needed somewhere
to live in, and there had to be a place for the administration. Some
agriculture was necessary to provide food for monks, priests and
pilgrims. Often the pilgrimage sanctuary was surrounded by a wall.

When local conditions made it possible, and the place of pilgrimage lay outside a city, large complexes could be constructed, as we can still see today from impressive examples.

2. Secular architecture

(a) City lay-outs

As a rule cities continued to exist, so their whole lay-out in late antiquity was governed by the building done at the time of the Roman empire. However, often parts of the original city territory were abandoned, and the new walls enclosed a much smaller area. The streets, squares and residential districts were taken over in all cases. Some of the great public buildings like theatres, amphitheatres, stadiums, market halls, baths and so on collapsed, but they were often also renovated, sometimes on a reduced scale. One example which is still impressive today is Ephesus with its streets, temples, baths, theatre, odeon and above all the private houses, which have constantly been renovated over the centuries.

There were various possibilities for extending or replanning cities in late antiquity. All are completely in the earlier tradition: we know of no innovations in the lay-outs of cities characteristic of late antiquity. In Constantinople the plans for the extension in 324/330 under Constantine and 408/413 under Theodosius II can only be read in part. However, it is striking that the great new squares which were laid out were arranged on the most important streets leading out of the cities.

In the newly founded city of Justiniana Prima (Caricin Grad, south of Nis), which was probably refounded in the sixth century, the streets follow the lie of the land. That was also usual with cities of the Greek and Roman period which lay in hilly country. The main public place is round; there are also earlier models for that, for example in Gerasa (Jordan). The churches are in prominent places, and the episcopal church has an important location. The advantages offered by rising land were also exploited in Zenobia on the Euphrates (in Syria), which was largely restored in the sixth century under the emperor Justinian. The city has an irregular shape: the walls describe a triangle. However, in the Euphrates plain attempts were made to apply a right-angled street system. The city of Sergiupolis (Resafa, in Syria) was refounded on its present site in the sixth century. It lies in the flat desert, so its basic form is a rectangle of the kind that was already used in the Roman imperial period for comparable cities. The streets seem to cross at right angles. The church buildings, which are particularly important in this place of pilgrimage, are in prominent sites, and occupy a relatively large amount of space.

(b) Public places, forums, triumphal columns and arches, streets

Public places and forums. In late antiquity the public places which were formed by important street intersections, and the forums (market places), were usually taken over from earlier times. Where necessary the earlier structures were repaired, but as a rule there was no occasion to build new ones. Exceptions are extensions or new foundations of cities, and building work which proved necessary after destructions, e.g. by an earthquake.

After the refounding and extension of Constantinople as the capital of the empire under Constantine the Great in 324/330, a forum was made as a new city centre. The sources indicate that it was round, but we know no details. There are models in the architecture of the imperial period (e.g. in Gerasa, Jordan). Only the porphyry column which stood at the centre has been preserved, though it is no longer its original height. The surrounding colonnades were richly decorated with statues, sometimes honorific statues and sometimes different kinds of earlier statues which had been brought to Constantinople.

Further out of the city, following the main street, at a later date four other public places were made, which were rectangular; however, these are no longer recognizable among the buildings of Istanbul. They were the Forum Tauri of Emperor Theodosius with columns and an arch (379–395), the Forum Bovis and the 'Philadelphion' (both of unknown date), and the forum of the emperor Arcadius with a high column (395–408).

In Justiniana Prima (Caricin Grad, south of Nis), which was refounded under the emperor Justinian in the sixth century, the main public place is round. In other cities, e.g. in Sergiupolis (Resafa, Syria) we know nothing of the arrangement of public places. In Dyrrachium (Durres, Albania) around 500 a large circular place was reconstructed in the centre of the city which was paved and surrounded by colonnades, probably at the crossing of the main streets. The arrangement probably goes back to the emperor Anastasius (491–518), who had his home city renewed at great expense and among other things also had new city walls built.

Triumphal columns and arches. These were also built in the early Christian period – as in the Roman imperial period – to celebrate victories of the emperor or other events. Larger-than-life statues of the emperors were put on the columns. In Constantinople mention should be made of Constantine's column, which originally consisted of nine smooth drums of porphyry, and was about 50 metres high; it had a high marble pedestal and bore a gilded bronze statue of the emperor; the Theodosius column (begun 386) and the Arcadius column (400/402 to 421), which in the tradition of the columns of the emperor Trajan (113 CE) and Marcus Aurelius (180/193) in Rome were decorated with spiral bands in relief (like their predecessors they celebrated victories of the emperor); and finally the simple Marcian column (450/452), the 'Gothic column' and a great column, parts of which are now in the Topkapi Saray and which probably bore the bronze statue of an emperor. Under the emperor Justinian the Augusteion, near Hagia Sophia in Constantinople, was restored and a high column erected on which from 543/44 a giant bronze equestrian statue (three to four times life-size) stood. A triumphal monument of another kind is still in its old place today in Constantinople, the central axis (*spina*) of the Hippodrome (pl.11.2; 27.3). This is the obelisk which was erected by the emperor Theodosius in 390 CE. The obelisk comes from Karnak in Egypt and is a work from around 1500 BCE; however, the base with reliefs was made for its erection in 390 CE.

In Ephesus there are four columns on the Arcadian Way (diag.28), the broad street leading from the theatre to the port; it is uncertain what they bore, but we are to assume that they

28. Sketch of the ceremonial street in Ephesus which leads from the theatre to the port ('Arcadian Way', c.400; overall length c.500 m; width 11 m).

were statues. A column was probably also erected at the circular place in Dyrrachium where remnants of a pedestal are still preserved.

Arches, which were erected above all for victories of emperors, but also for other occasions, were widespread in the time of the Roman empire. Mention might be made of the arches of the emperor Titus in Rome (81 CE), the emperor Trajan in Benevento (114 CE), the emperor Septimius Severus in Rome (203 CE), or the emperor Galerius in Thessaloniki (297–305 CE). In 312 CE the senate of Rome decreed an arch for Constantine the Great which is well preserved. Numerous earlier reliefs were reused; the heads of prominent figures, i.e. the emperors, were reworked into portraits of Constantine, and thus the arch was related to Constantine. Other reliefs were renovated, above all the narrow horizontal one on the upper parts. The arch celebrates the emperor's victory over Maxentius and shows e.g. the battle at the Milvian Bridge.

Such elaborate arches were evidently unusual at a later date.

Certainly the arch in the forum of Theodosius in Constantinople was quite large, but it was not decorated with reliefs. It should be noted that the columns, of which a series of fragments have been preserved, had the form of clubs held in hands. There are small arches e.g. in Ephesus in the 'Street of Curetes' (fourth/fifth century) or outside Corycus on the road to Elaeusa Sebaste (Cilicia, southern Turkey), but we do not know for what purpose they were erected.

Streets. No innovations in the streets within the cities can be detected in the early Christian period. Like those of the time of the Roman empire they had colonnades along the sides; there were gutters; and they were paved with large stones. In late antiquity, too, numerous triumphal statues were set up on them. Ephesus offers impressive examples. The very narrow Street of Curetes, which leads downwards from the place below the state agora, was renovated in the early Christian period, as is attested by the arch and the many pedestals of statues with inscriptions. The adjacent private houses, the Baths of Scholasticia, the temple of Hadrian and so on were also renovated. Under the emperor Arcadius (395–408), the street leading from the theatre to the harbour was splendidly developed (Arcadian Way, diag.28). It is 11 metres wide, around 500 metres long and had colonnades along the sides (the capitals, columns and pedestals are almost all made of earlier material which has been reused); an inscription tells us that by night it could be lit by fifty lanterns. Similar ceremonial streets will have existed in Constantinople and other cities of the empire. The 'Mesa', the main street of Constantinople, was partly fringed by two-storey colonnades in which numerous statues stood; there were workshops and shops in the rooms at the back. It is mentioned in various sources, but nothing is left of it today.

(c) City fortifications, fortresses

City fortifications. In the long period of peace in the second century and the majority of the third century CE the cities could get by without walls and strong fortifications as long as they were not near the frontiers of the empire. However, from the later third century the situation became increasingly unsafe, and in the course of time the cities had to be protected by walls around them. In 270/275 CE the emperor Aurelian had the powerful brick wall built in Rome which still impresses visitors today. Numerous structures from the fourth to sixth centuries are known throughout the Roman empire. Here it is possible only to refer to a few of them. There were different possibilities for fortifications.

In various ways the approximate earlier area of the city has been surrounded by a wall: Corycus, Hierapolis and Aphrodisias (Asia Minor) are examples. The walls usually consist of large square-cut stones, some of which come from earlier imperial buildings. Sometimes considerably earlier city walls have been used and improved without their course being essentially changed; that can be seen in Apameia in Syria and in Perga in Asia Minor (with a small extension to the south to include buildings from the imperial period). Very often, larger or smaller parts of the earlier city territory were given up, so that the cities were reduced in size. The new walls are made predominantly from the stones of earlier buildings which are no longer in use and have been torn down, and they were usually erected very hastily. That can be seen, for example, in Side or in Patara in Asia Minor and in Byllis in Albania. A popular practice was to utilize older, larger buildings in constructing new walls; these could be used as small fortresses. Thus on the east side of Patara the theatre, another large building (odeon, bouleuterion?), the gymnasium (?), baths and a temple have been incorporated into the new walls. The same thing can be seen e.g. in Side.

Rarely, cities have been enlarged and new walls built. The most famous and impressive example is the land wall of Constantinople which was built under emperor Theodosius between 408 and 413 (pl.12.1). It is the most powerful structure of its kind to have survived from late antiquity and protected the city, apart from some reinforcements in the Blachernae area, for more than a thousand years, until it was captured by the Ottomans in 1453. It consists of a moat, an outer wall and the main inner wall, and thus offers threefold protection with deep drops and a considerable increase in elevation. The towers have various forms and are put in gaps in the outer and inner walls. Importance was quite deliberately attached to an attractive appearance; layers of bright limestone blocks and bricks alternate, and the frameworks of doors and windows and the supporting arches are carefully built of brick. Thus the land wall of Constantinople is not only a prominent example of the military architecture of late antiquity but is also aesthetically appealing.

In the time of Justinian not only were a large number of fortifications reinforced throughout the empire, but several cities had new walls built. Here the construction was particularly careful. Examples are Justiniana Prima (Caricin Grad, south of Nis), Zenobia and Resafa in Syria.

In all these variations we can note that structurally the fortifications stand in the tradition of Graeco–Roman architecture. There seem to be no special features which we might regard as typical of late antiquity.

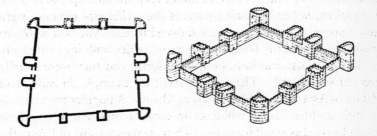

29. Fortress from late antiquity: ground-plan and sketch (Vig, northern Albania, mid-fourth century, c.115 x 100 m).

Fortresses. Fortresses were built to guard the frontiers of the empires and important roads in the interior. They are of different sizes and as a rule are rectangular or roughly square (diag.29); sometimes, however, they are also round or irregular, to fit the lie of the land. Their form, too, is in the tradition of the Roman imperial period. The corners are reinforced by thick towers, and further towers – rectangular or round – protect the sides. In smaller structures there are usually gates on two sides, each of which is protected by two towers; larger fortresses can have several gates. In North Africa, Syria (e.g. in the Hauran) and Jordan it is still possible to trace series of fortresses and recognize the architectural characteristics clearly; some examples have also been preserved in Albania (e.g. Vig, Elbasan, Paleocastra) and other areas of the Balkans or around Trier (e.g. Neumagen and Bitburg).

(d) Houses, villas, palaces, hippodromes, bishops' palaces, inns

Houses, villas. Only a very few houses from the early Christian period have been preserved in the cities. There do not seem to have been any new forms. Houses several storeys high with apartments for rent in Rome and Ostia were still being used in late antiquity, and there is no evidence of large-scale rebuilding. The private houses in Ephesus give a good idea of homes in antiquity. However, they come from the earlier period of the empire and have been renovated, rebuilt and restored over centuries, so they are not examples of house buildings from late antiquity. Phases of rebuilding in late antiquity can also be noted in various grander houses in Ostia. More

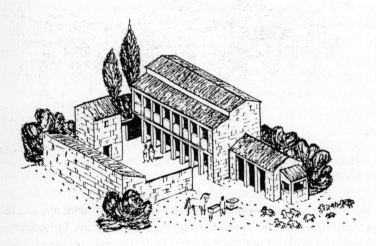

30. Country house in north-west Syria (fourth/fifth century): sketch.

modest houses have been excavated e.g. in Corinth and Philippi. However, no special features can be recognized; the forms are in the earlier tradition.

The tradition is better for houses and smaller villas in the country. Numerous houses and farmsteads are particularly well known from two areas of the Roman empire, from 'Rough Cilicia' (southern Turkey) and north–western Syria (pl.30). However, there is no comprehensive treatment of forms of buildings which could allow us to draw conclusions about life in late antiquity. The houses seem to have been built with an excellent walling technique: in Syria from large stones which were carefully cut, in Cilicia from smaller quarry stones and mortar, and square-cut stone for prominent places. They often have two storeys. The rooms are of different sizes, some of them open to the outside; they have colonnades in front, sometimes with two storeys. Store rooms can be in the house or in separate buildings.

31. Konz on the Moselle (near Trier): sketch of the imperial summer villa, from the north (mid-fourth century, size about 84 x 38 m).

There are various forms in larger villas, all of which stand in the tradition of earlier buildings. In Piazza Armerina in Sicily (early fourth century), the rooms are grouped round a courtyard (peristyle) surrounded by colonnades in a grandiose way. By contrast, the villa in Konz near Trier (diag.31), in which there is evidence that Emperor Valentinian lived in the summer of 371 and signed four decrees, in other words which was an imperial summer villa, is an enclosed complex with protruding sides and colonnades (villa with corner projections and portico). This type was very widespread in late antiquity and is also depicted on mosaics. It probably also included the villa of Welschbillig near Trier, which was built or thoroughly renovated around 375. On the main axis of the building it has a large basin for water around which there are galleries of herms, most of which have been preserved. Perhaps the substantial complex in Akkale (Cilicia, southern Turkey) also represents the type of villa with corner projections and portico. It is not far from the water, and up above there would have been a splendid view of the sea from an arcade. Other villas take the form of a small fortress, e.g. Pfalzel near Trier (fourth century), or are built like castles with walls round them. The most famous example is the complex which the emperor Diocletian had built in Spalato (Split, Dalmatia) as a home for his old age. The emperor abdicated in 305, and the palatial villa will have been built shortly beforehand. It is in an excellent state of preservation, as later a city was built in it. The complex in Gamzigrad in Serbia (Felix Romuliana) is also a large walled villa, but not laid out in such a regular way as Spalato. It seems to be the complex which Emperor Galerius (died 311) had provided for himself in his old age. There are earlier predecessors; the splendid rebuilding may have taken place after 305. It is striking that all these villas have a prominent room, sometimes elongated with an apse. In regions in which the climate required it, it could even be heated. This is a splendid reception room, which was often of a considerable size and modelled on the corresponding rooms in imperial palaces. Furthermore, the villa complex also had baths.

Palaces. A distinction can be made between private palaces and imperial palaces. There are the remains of three private palaces in Constantinople, and another in Ephesus, which can give a good idea. There was no pattern for the buildings. In imitation of the imperial palaces, all had a prominent, splendidly decorated reception room of a considerable size, but differing in form: round, with niches inside (Bodrum palace, fourth century; and the Palace of Lausus, beginning of fifth century, in Constantinople); hexagon with conches (Palace of Antiochus, built 416–418; in the sixth century the church of St Euphemia was erected in this hall, in Constantinople); an octagon inscribed in a square, with conches in the diagonals and a prominent apse (Ephesus, fifth century?). These rooms were vaulted with cupolas; this can be inferred from the unusual strength of the walls. In Ephesus the complex includes numerous other rooms and a bath. Furthermore, there is a long entrance hall in front of the palace, which was possibly built in different phases. There seems to have been a large garden with rounded sides in the Antiochus palace, with the rooms running alongside it.

In many large cities of the empire there were palaces for the emperor(s), for example in Rome, Constantinople, Milan, Ravenna, Thessaloniki, Nicomedia, Antioch, Sirmium and Trier. Various remains have survived, so that some special features can be detected. The model for all the structures was the palace of the Roman emperors on the Palatine in Rome. The imperial palaces of late antiquity are not enclosed monumental buildings either. Rather, they occupy a considerable amount of space, within which the buildings which served the public, private areas, churches and gardens were loosely divided. A large representative reception room with a prominent apse, in which the throne for the emperor was put, was a regular feature of them. It was richly decorated with marble floors and wall-coverings. The 'basilica' in Trier (early fourth century CE), which was probably the audience hall of the imperial palace (diag.32; pl.11.1), gives us some idea of it. The remains of a room of the same shape and size have also been found in Thessaloniki. There will have been further buildings in the grounds of the imperial palace for smaller receptions. These include the peristyle courtyard, parts of which have been excavated in Constantinople: rectangular colonnades surround a garden court; on one side there is a prominent room with an apse; tesselated mosaics decorate the floor, and marble panels the walls. In Thessaloniki, alongside the long rectangular building with an apse there is another octagonal room with a cupola, which also has an apse and is decorated with outstanding panel mosaics on the floor and the walls. In Antioch the imperial palace was on an island on the Orontes. It included the large, probably octagonal, church founded by Constantine. In Constantinople, the 'Great Church', the predecessor of Hagia Sophia, borders on the imperial palace. In Trier the double church, today the cathedral and Church of the Virgin, was built only later, probably after 326, in the precinct of the imperial palace. Here, an earlier complex of buildings was destroyed, which included the banqueting hall with ceiling paintings (these, however, have been splendidly preserved); this room may have belonged to the imperial palace.

32. Trier, 'basilica': ground plan of the imperial palace hall (without the annexe; the apse is to the north, early fourth century, length c.74 m); cf. pl.11.1.

In addition, large baths were built in the area of the imperial palace, which were open to the public. One example is the imperial baths in Trier (diag.34). In Thessaloniki the remains of a theatre have been found in the area of the imperial palace. Furthermore, the triumphal arch of the emperor Galerius and a round temple (present-day Hagios Georgios) were incorporated into the palace complex.

Hippodromes (Circuses). Hippodromes were regularly part of imperial palaces. The model was Rome, where the Circus Maximus lies below the palace on the Palatine. In Constantinople, Antioch, Thessaloniki, Sirmium, Milan and probably also Trier, the combination of palace and hippodrome was taken over. In the hippodrome the emperor provided entertainment for the people and appeared to his subjects, high up in a box; he could be given an ovation, but the people also had the opportunity to express its disapproval. The structure in Constantinople can give some idea of the splendid decoration of a hippodrome (pl.11.2). First, we have descriptions, and secondly there are still three monuments on the central axis (*spina*): the obelisk erected in 390 CE under Theodosius; the Serpentine Column which was erected after the victory over the

Persians at Salamis in 480 CE and in 479 CE at Plataea by the Greeks in the sanctuary of Apollo, and was brought by Constantine to his capital; and a stone pillar, which possibly dates from the fourth century CE and, as can be inferred from an inscription, was renovated in the tenth century with gilded bronze panels (the old sheathing had been destroyed in the iconoclastic controversy). The reliefs on the pedestal of the obelisk, some of which show the box with the imperial family, give an idea of the celebrations in the hippodrome (pl.27.3).

Episcopal palaces. The residences of bishops, a considerable number of which are known, form a special group. They are near to the main churches in the city concerned. The arrangement of rooms differs greatly and is connected with local circumstances, but some common characteristics can be identified. As a rule the main feature in the complex is a larger room which served as a reception room – as in the imperial palaces and in large profane villas. This was usually an aisleless room with an apse, but sometimes a centralized room which was probably vaulted. As far as we can see from the remains, this reception room had particularly splendid decorations; so the bishops vied with the emperors and high military and civil dignitaries. Sometimes there are storerooms with large vessels (for grain, oil and wine, e.g. in Philippi). A bath can also form part of the complex (e.g. in Philippi). Outwardly the bishops' palaces do not seem to have been particularly prominent, and elaborate façades are unknown. Here, too, they correspond to other palaces. However, some of the extant examples are quite large.

Inns. Very little is known of the 'hotels' of the early Christian period. There were certainly such buildings in the larger cities and in pilgrimage sanctuaries. Some buildings have survived in north–west Syria which were evidently inns (e.g. in Deir Siman, below Qalat Siman, pl.10.2). They have several storeys and a series of rooms which are sometimes accessible from outside, from a covered passage.

(e) Aqueducts, cisterns, fountains, baths

Aqueducts. Water was – and is! – a necessity for human life. Especially in the cities there were problems over supplying water in sufficient quantity. Only in exceptional cases were there productive springs within the walls. As a rule cisterns had to be made in which the rainwater of individual houses could be collected. Very occasionally, already in the Greek period there seem to have been watercourses which carried water over long distances into a city. There are examples in Pergamon, including one which is 42 kilometres long.

The Romans were masters of engineering. Extended structures were built in numerous cities to convey water. Where possible they followed the lie of the land and were laid underground. Thus for example we can trace a watercourse of 95.3 km which led from the Eifel to Cologne. If necessary, smaller or larger valleys were spanned by bridge-like constructions (aqueducts). Sometimes these were massive structures, as near Rome, at the Pont du Gard near Nîmes, or in Segovia.

In late antiquity the watercourses and aqueducts continued to be maintained: repairs were made where needed and they were also rebuilt where necessary. One example which is still impressive today is the aqueduct in Constantinople (Istanbul) which was built in the time of the emperor Valens (263–278) in order to bridge the valley between two hills (pl.12.2). The watercourse brought water over considerable distances from the hill country north-west of the city and ended at the forum which the Emperor Theodosius had built. Other examples of well-preserved aqueducts which have been built or repaired in late antiquity can be found at Elaeusa Sebaste ('Rough Cilicia', in Southern Turkey).

Cisterns. In the cities the water was collected in cisterns. Certainly many houses, palaces and the monasteries also had their own cisterns in late antiquity. However, frequently the cities made provision for the water supply in large cisterns. Sometimes these were open structures. Three can still be seen in Istanbul, of a quite enormous size. There was also a large open cistern in Amphipolis in northern Greece. Further examples are the open cisterns in Meriamlik, Seleuceia and Corycus in 'Rough Cilicia'; the one in Corycus unusually has an irregular ground plan and most of it is not sunk in the rock; substantial walls have been built.

Covered cisterns cost more to make, but protected the water better. Some of them are among the most brilliant achievements of the architecture of late antiquity, like the Yerebatan Saray cistern

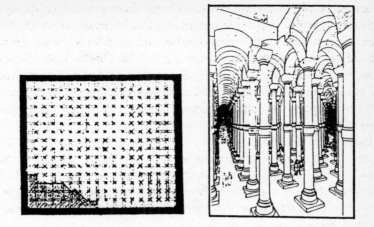

33. Subterranean cistern, Binbirderek ('1001 pillars') in Istanbul: ground plan and sketch of interior (fifth/sixth century, c.64 x 56.4 m, capacity around 40,000 cubic metres).

(subterranean castle) and Binbirdirek ('1001 pillars', diag.33) cistern in Istanbul, which was probably made in the sixth century under the emperor Justinian. Structures in other places are smaller but sometimes very impressive, for example in the splendid 'fortress' of Akkale and in the pilgrimage sanctuary of Meriamlik (both in 'Rough Cilicia'), in Dara (south–east Turkey) or in Resafa (Syria).

Fountains. Often water appears to have been made available to the population at public fountains. Such structures already appear in the Greek period and then more frequently in the Roman period. Several are attested by literary mentions from late antiquity and some have been investigated. In Constantinople, for example, there must have been a large fountain in the Theodosius forum at the end of the Valens aqueduct, but it is lost. Smaller fountains have been preserved in Ephesus and give a good idea of purpose-built buildings of this kind. The pipes in the back wall led water into a basin; it was contained at the back by panels with various kinds of decoration; water could be drawn from the basin.

Baths. In the time of the Roman empire the public baths were very important, and remained so into late antiquity. Furthermore, new ones were built and older structures which had been damaged for various reasons were renewed. There were small baths in private houses, palaces, hospitals, and sometimes also in monasteries; in the cities more or less major complexes were open to all. Where new buildings were erected, they did not differ from the earlier buildings of the imperial period. We have no idea of the nature of those built by Constantine in Rome and Constantinople, and none of the buildings of Justinian mentioned by Procopius seem to have been preserved.

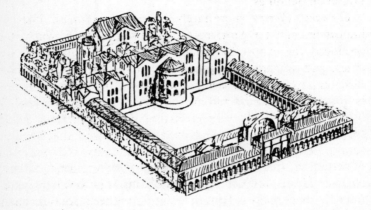

34. Large baths complex: sketch of the planned first state of the 'Imperial Baths' in Trier (c.300, overall dimensions c.250 x 145 m).

In many cases, however, we can see reconstructions or renovations of older baths. Examples are the harbour baths and the baths of Scholasticia in Ephesus, the baths in Carthage or the imperial baths in Trier. The Trier structure (diag.34) is the largest in the Roman empire; it was built after 293 CE and after a lengthy interruption was finished under the emperor Valentinian I (364–75), in a much reduced form; it then, however, probably served as a throne room rather than as a bath.

(f) Market basilicas, shops, granaries, oil presses

Market basilicas. Nothing is known of these buildings, though there must have been large numbers of them in cities. So far no market basilica built or largely restored in the early period has been found. We merely have a few references in the sources. There do not seem to have been new forms.

Shops. In Sardes (western Turkey), a series of workshops and shops have been excavated. They were built on the outside of the large complex which in late antiquity comprised the baths, the gymnasium and the synagogue, and opened on to the important through street. Even today they give a vivid impression of such utilitarian buildings.

Granaries (*horrea*, more rarely *horreum*; *granarium*). They were important, first for gathering grain in the areas in which it was produced for export to Rome, Constantinople and other large cities, and secondly, for keeping it in the larger cities prior to distribution. Enormous structures from the time of the empire can be found e.g. in Patara and in Andriake (south-west Turkey). The building in Andriake was erected under the emperor Hadrian (probably after 129 CE) and used at least until the late fourth century CE, as an inscription from the years 388/392 attests. However, it is not known whether there were reconstructions or changes in late antiquity. The granaries in the two places are next to the harbour and were meant for gathering grain from the interior and storing it for transport to Rome and later to Constantinople. In Corasium (Cilicia, southern Turkey), the remains of a narrow and extended building were preserved which in late antiquity was built directly on to the harbour. It will have served as a harbour warehouse (now destroyed).

In Rome, Constantinople or Ravenna the granaries have been lost and we only have references in the sources. The remains which were excavated in Trier and can be reconstructed in drawings (early fourth century, diag.35) give some idea of granaries in late antiquity. This was a large complex next to the port on the Moselle. It consists of two long two-storey parallel halls with a courtyard between them. The exterior was divided by blind arches, and so the building not only fulfilled its purpose as a granary but was a representative complex worthy of the imperial residence.

Oil presses. These are known above all from Cilicia (southern Turkey) and the limestone region of north-west Syria. However, only the recesses in the rock have been preserved. From these it is

35. Granary (*horrea*): sketch of the structure in Trier (fourth century: size c.80 x 54 m).

possible to reconstruct some structures. There do not seem to have been any special architectural features in the oil-presses of antiquity.

(g) Trunk roads, bridges

Trunk roads. The Romans had opened up their enormous empire by a developed network of roads which served administrative, economic and military purposes. In late antiquity maintenance seems largely to have continued. Only rarely have parts been preserved which can be dated with some certainty to late antiquity, for example in 'Rough Cilicia' and in northern Syria. These roads have no special features. There is a layer of relatively thick slabs of different sizes which were probably laid in a bed of rubble or gravel. Sometimes they seem only to have been fortified country roads.

Bridges. The roads also had bridges for crossing streams, rivers and marshy land. It is only rarely possible to demonstrate building activity from late antiquity in what has come down to us, both repairs and new structures. One example is the 'Roman Bridge' in Trier over the Moselle (around 370 metres long with twelve arches); it was built in 454 CE, was in use in late antiquity and the Middle Ages, and even now carries modern traffic. Improvements were probably made in late antiquity, when Trier was an imperial residence; however, we cannot demonstrate them in the present-day structure. A very long but not very high bridge, the remains of which are to be found east of Limyra (south-west Turkey, originally around 360 metres long with 28 arches), could date from late antiquity.

Under the emperor Justinian the network of roads was also developed, new bridges were built and earlier ones repaired. Such measures can be demonstrated e.g. in Tarsus, Adana and Mopsuestia in south-eastern Turkey and in the bridge over the Sangarios (length c.420 m) in north-western Turkey. No special features typical of late antiquity can be seen in the bridges; the forms of construction are completely in the older Roman tradition.

III

Burials

General. No specifically Christian burials can be demonstrated from the first two centuries anywhere; in large parts of the Roman empire there are also none from the third or even from the fourth century CE. The form of burials will not have differed from that of the pagan population. There were great differences within the Roman provinces. In Rome in the early empire it was customary to cremate the dead and put the ashes in urns or niches of a tomb. The poor whose relatives could not afford the cost of cremation were presumably wrapped in a cloth and buried in the ground in the area of a cemetery without any special marking for the place. A somewhat more elaborate form of burial was to use one or more interlocked earthenware vessels for the corpse or to cover it with shards of pottery or roof tiles. There are examples of such relatively elaborate possibilities in Ostia, but they will have been quite widespread. There are no offerings which could indicate any veneration of the dead. It must for the moment remain open whether initially the Christians also cremated their dead; the sources are unclear, but predominantly suggest this.

Around 110/120 CE a slow change in customs can be noted in Rome. Increasingly the dead are no longer cremated but put in sarcophagi. For most Christians of the time, however, these may have been too expensive. Only in the late third century in Rome do the first sarcophagi with Christian depictions begin. From around 200 CE in Rome we have increased indications that Christians no longer wanted to be buried with pagan relatives and neighbours but in their own cemeteries; in other areas of the Roman empire the tradition only begins much later. It is no longer the wider family or the patron who is responsible for burying the poor, but the Christian community under its bishop. Around 200 CE a deacon, Calixtus, evidently received a commission from Zephyrinus, bishop of Rome, to organize a *coemeterium* (cemetery) for the Christian community; this had now increased considerably and included a large number of poor people. In this way the first catacombs came into being. It was impossible for the community to buy any extensive land for financial reasons. They had to use a very small surface area, and thus go deep into the earth. We do not know whether this land was bought by the Roman Christian community or given by a rich member. Later there are subterranean tomb chambers and also tombs on the surface which were intended for individual families.

Special structures were erected for honouring martyrs, sometimes above their graves, but sometimes also without any direct connection with them.

Catacombs. The nature of the ground around Rome offers unusually favourable possibilities of digging deep tombs, since it consists of volcanic stone of a considerable thickness which can easily be worked. Pagan families had already made small subterranean tombs (*hypogea*) at various places outside the city walls. Now around 200 CE large subterranean complexes were made for the Christian community with passages and cross-passages (pl.16.1, the Catacomb of Priscilla). Hollows were made in the walls one above another for the burials (*loculi*, 'small places'), which were sealed with bricks or slabs. Such a subterranean area was called *coemeterium* (from the Greek *koimao*, sleep, Latin *coemeterium*, cemetery); today we use the expression 'catacombs', after the name of a Roman meadow *ad*

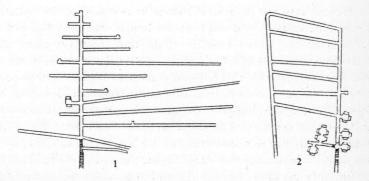

36. Sketch of the catacombs in Rome: 1. branch system; 2. grid system.

catacumbas ('by the hollow') for an area on the Appian Way near S.Sebastiano. These catacombs may be regarded as typical of Christians, and above all of Rome, since only there did the necessary conditions come together: there was stone which could easily be worked; space for tombs was rare and dear, but the Christian community had to accommodate as many dead bodies as cheaply as possible and using minimum space; the organization of the community made it possible to extend the structure considerably.

We now know of around 60 catacombs of different sizes in Rome: between 150 and 175 kilometres of passages have been opened up with an estimated 750,000 tombs and 25,000 epitaphs. Two types of catacombs can be distinguished, but are frequently combined: 1. the 'branch' system in which side passages of different length branch off the one main passage (diag.36.1) and 2. the grid system, in which at least two roughly parallel passages running lengthways are joined together in a grid by cross passages (diag.36.2). If additional space was needed, it was possible to deepen the existing passages. However, whole systems with new passages could also be made under the older ones. It was important even underground to remain within the limits of the piece of land. The passages were as a rule very narrow, but therefore high. Somewhat more prosperous families had special tomb chambers made within the system of passages (*cubicula*, pl.16.2; catacombs of the Via Latina), sometimes with sarcophagi or with burial places in niches (*arcosolia*). A special chamber for the Popes was provided within the passage system of the Calixtus Catacomb, the Papal Crypt, in which the first burials were probably made in 235/36 CE. Initially it will have been very simple; it was probably decorated with columns and large inscriptions in the second half of the fourth century under Pope Damasus.

A little later, after the Calixtus catacombs, the catacombs of Priscilla, Praetextatus and Domitilla were made. These had private subterranean tombs as a starting point; other catacombs, including some Jewish ones, followed. There were burials in the Roman catacombs from around 200 until shortly after 400 CE. One of the latest complexes is the catacomb on the Via Latina (or Via Dino Compagni), which was decorated with high-quality wall paintings around 370/380 (pls.16.2, 18.2). After the invasion of Rome by the West Goths under Alaric in 410, the catacombs were largely abandoned, and new wall paintings were only put in a very few places.

The catacombs of Rome are important for early Christian art for several reasons: the tomb chambers – not the passages – are often decorated with wall paintings; thus a unique treasury of paintings from the years between 200 and 400 has been preserved in Rome (cf.IV.1). Objects have been pressed in the mortar of the seals of the *loculi* as identification marks, e.g. coins, the bases of gold glass (cf.VI.6), complete glass objects and lamps (cf.VI.9); moreover, numerous lamps have been found, which were needed in the dark passages. A large number of the slabs sealing the *loculi* have not only an inscription but in addition a figured representation, usually engraved and only rarely in relief (cf. Ch.V.2); so we have further evidence of early Christian and sometimes even pre-Constantinian pictorial art which has been preserved in the catacombs. Sarcophagi were put in what seem to be the relatively few tomb chambers; these are often in a particularly good state of preservation (cf. Ch.V.1).

Outside Rome there are few comparable sites. Examples are: S.Gennaro in Naples (important for its paintings and mosaics); S.Cristina in Bolsena; the catacombs in Sicily (above all in Syracuse), on Malta and in western North Africa; and the subterranean tomb complex on the Greek island of Melos. The Jewish 'catacombs' of Beth-Shearim are older than the Roman catacombs

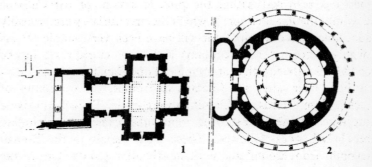

37. Ground plans of tomb shrines from late antiquity: 1. 'Mausoleum of Galla Placidia', Ravenna (c.450; length c.15 m), cf. pl.17.1; 2. S.Costanza, Mausoleum of Constantina, daughter of Constantine the Great, at S.Agnese in Rome (middle of fourth century; inner diameter 22.5 m); cf. pl.4.

but are not comparable with them, because they have quite a different form; thus they are not to be seen as forerunners of the Roman structures.

Subterranean tombs. On various occasions the Christians took over earlier forms of subterranean burials, namely small chamber tombs, the walls of which are painted in several cases (e.g. in Thessaloniki, Nicaea–Iznik, Kayseri), or rather larger tomb chambers, sometimes also with paintings (e.g. Alexandria).

Tombs above ground. Only a few well-to-do people and the imperial family could afford such buildings. Their forms are completely in the earlier Roman tradition. The preference is for round buildings with cupolas. Examples are the Tor Pignattara at SS.Marcellino e Pietro in Rome, which Constantine the Great probably originally planned as his own tomb and in which his mother Helena was then buried later (c.320/330); the mausoleum of the emperor Honorius at St Peter's, Rome (c.410/420); the mausoleum of Constantina, the daughter of Constantine the Great, present-day S.Costanza, a round building with an ambulatory, probably modelled on the Anastasis Rotunda in Jerusalem (c.350; pl.37.2; pl.40), probably the mausoleum which Constantine the Great had built for himself at the Church of the Apostles in Constantinople. The so-called mausoleum of Galla Placidia in Ravenna is cruciform (c.450, diag.37.1; pl.17.1); it was probably a tomb. The mausoleum of

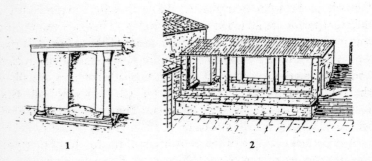

38. Memorials for martyrs in Rome: 1. memorial of St Peter under St Peter's (c.200); 2. 'triclia' under S.Sebastiano; hall for commemorative festivals for Peter and Paul (mentioned in 258 and in use to around 320).

Theoderic in Ravenna is a two-storey centralized building of an unusual form (beginning of the sixth century). Finally, mention should be made of the mausoleum of Centcelles in Spain, which has been built in the room of a villa; it is conjectured that it was intended for Constantine's son, Constans, who was murdered in 350 CE, but that is not certain. The Cella Trichora, a triconch in the area of the Calixtus Catacomb in Rome (c.300?), and the splendid square mausoleum of El Bara in North Syria, which has a roof in the form of a pyramid and contains several sarcophagi (c.500, pl.17.2), might be mentioned as examples of large tombs of rich private persons.

Memorials for martyrs. The veneration of martyrs begins in the second century. The earliest information we have is about the tomb of Bishop Polycarp of Smyrna (present-day Izmir, Turkey). However, in the time before Constantine it was evidently not possible to build elaborate and prominent tombs and decorate them architecturally. Thus around 200 CE the tombs of Peter (diag.38.1) and Paul in Rome will have been quite modest. Later, they were then decorated with increasing splendour. At the end of the third century – the dating is not certain – a square building may have been built over the tomb of John in Ephesus (diag.39). After Constantine the Great the tombs which were venerated were decorated in an elaborate way and sometimes incorporated into the churches (e.g. in St Peter's, diag.5, and probably also St Paul in Rome and the Church of St John in Ephesus, diag.16). Often mausoleums of different forms are attached to the churches. There are examples of this in almost all areas of the Mediterranean. However, in most cases we do not know for whom these buildings were intended. In Syria and Palestine there is often an annexe alongside the apse, usually on the south side, in which reliquaries (cf. Ch.V.2) were put. Such installations can also be seen in several churches of Cilicia, even where reliquaries have not been found.

An unusual example of the veneration of the tombs of martyrs is the Necropolis of the Seven Sleepers at Ephesus: since the late fourth century the legend of the seven young men has been attached to a large complex of caves, and – above all in the fifth and sixth century – this complex was developed as a burial place with numerous tombs, a large mausoleum and at least one church. A

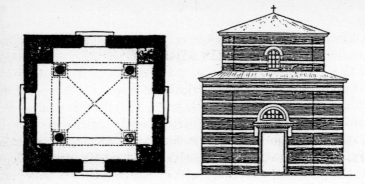

39. Building over the tomb of St John at Ephesus: ground plan and sketch (c.300 or fourth century?, dimensions around 18.50 x 18.50 m), cf. pl.16.

unique and highly significant structure has been found under S.Sebastiano on the Appian Way (diag.38.2). It was used for commemorations of Peter and Paul, the princes of the apostles, as we can see from numerous graffiti on the walls. Several sources also indicate this. There was a large open space, a roofed hall (*triclia*), a fountain and other small buildings. The complex was already standing in 258 (or 260 CE) and it remained in use until the building of the large basilica, probably until c.350 CE. Thus it is the earliest memorial to martyrs of which there is archaeological evidence. We do not know why Peter and Paul were venerated at this place, since there is no indication that any kind of relics were taken there. Moreover the church, which is dedicated to both princes of the apostles (Basilica Apostolorum), bears no relation to the earlier structure, which is totally covered with rubble.

IV

Paintings and Mosaics

In the Greek and especially in the Roman period, people were surrounded with pictures. There were wall paintings and stuccos, and also some wall and ceiling mosaics in private houses, tombs and public buildings; and the floors were decorated with mosaics. Pictures were widespread, as were illustrated manuscripts.

At first, Christians were opposed to pictures. They strictly observed the prohibition of images in the Old Testament: 'You shall not make for yourself a graven image or any likeness of anything that is in heaven above, or that is in the earth beneath, or that is in the water under the earth; you shall not bow down to them or serve them' (Exod.20.4f.); 'You shall make for yourselves no idols and erect no graven image or pillar, and you shall not set up a figured stone in your land, to bow down to them; for I am the Lord your God' (Lev.26.1; cf. Deut.4.16–18). But from around 200 CE the Graeco-Roman tradition, which was well disposed to imagery, slowly prevailed against the Old Testament prohibition of images, first of all in the private sphere but soon also in churches: there are far more pictures in the late third century, and in the fourth century they are usual everywhere. This transition also becomes clear in numerous statements in the literature of the early Christian period (cf. the bibliographies in Ch.VIII).

Tombs and church buildings were painted or decorated with tesselated mosaics, rarely also with figured panel mosaics; mosaics were also put down on parts of the floors. In some areas of the Roman empire mosaics were even used as panels for tombs. At a relatively early stage there seem also to have been images on panels and manuscripts with figured illustrations. In addition there are sarcophagi and small works of art of various kinds.

The tradition in paintings and mosaics is inadequate and uneven. A large number of wall paintings have been preserved in the Roman catacombs, including some from the time before Constantine, but in the other areas of the empire there is virtually nothing in tombs. However, the few remains, which are widely scattered, show that there were numerous tombs with paintings. Only in exceptional cases have churches of the early period come down to us with a reasonably substantial part of the original paintings or mosaics intact; most have been rebuilt or destroyed in the course of the centuries.

The tradition is better in floor mosaics. In churches which have been renovated and are still used for worship today, the floor has usually also been changed, but often earlier levels have been found under later floors. In churches which have been destroyed over the course of centuries, the floor has usually been left, even where the stone material from the walls has largely been plundered and reused. Thus numerous mosaics have been exposed in excavations. So our knowledge of floor mosaics is better than that of paintings and mosaics on the walls.

No panel paintings whatsoever have been preserved from the early Christian period. We can merely see from various references that they existed from the third century on. Only a very few remnants of illustrated early Christian manuscripts have been handed down; here, too, we can infer that they were once numerous.

1. Wall paintings

Churches, tombs and profane buildings sometimes had wall paintings in the early Christian period. However, only a few fragments remain, so it is not certain when they begin. The earliest known to us appear in the baptistery of the house church of Dura Europos (eastern Syria, by the Euphrates, 232/233 BCE; diag.34, pl.1.1). These are pictures from the New Testament and the Old Testament which seem to be sections from a cycle. The scenes were certainly not 'invented' for this remote church; rather, there will already have been churches with extensive wall paintings in the major centres early in the third century. The next reference in time comes from around 306: a local synod in Elvira (Spain) prohibited wall paintings with biblical themes in churches. Such a prohibition

Plate 1

1. Dura Europos, baptistery of the house church (232/3–256)

2. Jerusalem, rotunda of the Holy Sepulchre, looking north-west
(seventeenth-century engraving)

Plate 2

1. Rome, S.Sabina, from the south-east (422–432)

2. Rome, S.Sabina, looking east (422–432)

Plate 3

1. Ravenna, S.Apollinare in Classe, from the north-west (540/550)

2. Ravenna, S.Apollinare Nuovo, looking west (beginning of sixth century)

Plate 4

1. Rome, S.Constanza, from the north-east (c.350)

2. Rome, S.Constanza, looking south-west (c.350)

Plate 5

1. Rome, S.Stefano Rotondo, from the south (468–483)

2. Rome, S.Stefano Rotondo, interior (468–483)

Plate 6

1. Butrint (Albania), basilica, from the south-east (early sixth century)

2. Butrint, basilica, looking east (early sixth century and later)

Plate 7

1. Alahan Monastir, eastern church from the south-east (c.500)

2. Hierapolis, north baths, looking north-east (second century and sixth century?)

Plate 8

1. Salah (south-eastern Turkey), Mar Yakub, from the west (c.500)

2. Resafa (Syria), basilica A, looking north-east (early sixth century)

Plate 9

1. Qalat Siman, monastery of St Simeon, south façade (480/490)

2. Qalat Siman, octagon with St Simeon's pillar, looking north

Plate 10

1. Butrint (Albania), baptistery, from the south (early sixth century)

2. Deir Siman (north Syria), inn or house (fifth/sixth century)

Plate 11

1. Trier, 'basilica', from the north-west (early fourth century)

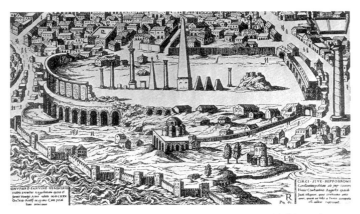

2. Constantinople/Istanbul, view of the palace area with hippodrome from the east (engraving c.1600)

Plate 12

1. Constantinople/Istanbul, land wall (408–413)

2. Constantinople/Istanbul, aqueduct of Valens (364/378)

Plate 13

1. Ravenna, S.Francesco,
Corinthian capital with transom
(second half of fifth century)

2. Silifke, museum,
composite capital
(second half of fifth century)

3. Lechaion (near Corinth),
composite capital
(second half of fifth century)

4. Lechaion (near Corinth),
Ionic transom capital (c.500)

Plate 14

1. Ravenna, Piazza del Popolo, capital with 'windswept' leaves (c.500)

2. Tirana, historical museum, two-zone capital (from Dyrrachium, c.500)

3. Istanbul, garden of Hagia Sophia, ambo with two staircases (sixth century)

Plate 15

1. Rome, S.Clemente, barrier panel
(sixth century)

2. Ravenna, S.Apollinare Nuovo,
barrier panel (sixth century)

3. Ravenna, Museo Nationale, barrier panel
(sixth century)

Plate 16

1. Rome, passage in the Catacomb of Priscilla

2. Rome, cubiculum (tomb chamber) in the Catacomb
of the Via Latina

Plate 17

1. Ravenna, 'Mausoleum of Galla Placidia', from the west (c.450)

2. El Bara (northern Syria), tomb (c.500)

Plate 18

1. Rome, Catacomb of SS.Marcellino e Pietro, ceiling picture including depictions of Jonah (middle of fourth century)

2. Rome, Catacomb of the Via Latina, wall painting with Heracles leading Alcestis from the underworld (second half of fourth century)

Plate 19

1. Vatican, tomb M under
St Peter's, wall mosaic with
ascension of Christ (c.300)

2. Hinton (England),
floor mosaic with bust of Christ
(fourth century)

3. Rome, S.Costanza, mosaic with the 'giving of the law', eastern apse
(c.350)

Plate 20

1. Ravenna, S.Apollinare Nuovo, mosaic with the raising of Lazarus (early sixth century)

2. Thessaloniki, Hagios Georgios, cupola mosaic with architecture and saints (c.500)

Plate 21

1. Rome, S.Pudenziana, apse mosaic with Christ and the apostles (c.400)

2. Ravenna, S.Apollinare in Classe, apse mosaic with transfiguration of Christ (c.550)

Plate 22

1. Ostia, house at the Porta Marina, wall panel mosaic with Christ (late fourth century)

2. Mar Gabriel (south-east Turkey), floor panel mosaic (c.500)

Plate 23

1. Butrint (Albania), baptistery, floor mosaic (sixth century)

2. Durres-Arapaj (Albania), basilica, floor mosaic
(middle of sixth century)

Plate 24

1. Rome, Museo Nazionale Romano, sarcophagus
(c.320)

2. Vatican, St Peter, sarcophagus of Junius Bassus (c.359)

3. Ravenna, S.Apollinare in Classe, sarcophagus
(c.450)

Plate 25

1. Istanbul, Archaeological Museum,
'Sarcophagus of the Princes'
(late fourth century)

2. Istanbul, Archaeological Museum,
'Pseudo-sarcophagus' (fifth century)

3. Istanbul, Archaeological Museum,
decorative sarcophagus (late fourth century)

Plate 26

1. Trier, Rheinisches Landesmuseum, sarcophagus
(first half of fourth century)

2. Afyon (Turkey), museum, decorative sarcophagus (591/2)

3. Qanawat (southern Syria), 'Seraglio', sarcophagus
(fifth century?)

Plate 27

1. Ravenna, Museo Arcivescovile, reliquary
(middle of fifth century)

2. Urbino, Archaeological Museum, tomb slab of
Eutropos (from Rome, c.300)

3. Istanbul, Hippodrome, pedestal of the obelisk
of Theodosius (390)

Plate 28

1. Istanbul, Archaeological Museum, statue of the emperor Valentinian in a toga (c.390)

2. Istanbul, Archaeological Museum, statue of an official in a chlamys (early fifth century)

3. Paris, Louvre, silver reliquary (fifth century)

Plate 29

1. Berlin, Staatsbibliothek, ivory diptych of Probianus (after 395)

2. Berlin, Museum für Spätantike und Byzantinische Kunst, panel of an ivory diptych with the enthroned Mother of God (middle of the sixth century)

3. Trier, Rheinisches Landesmuseum, ivory pyx (second half of fifth century)

Plate 30

1. Bursa, museum, tombstone (late third century)

2. Ravenna, Museo Nazionale, relief with Heracles (fifth/sixth century)

3. Munich, Bavaria, National-museum, weight for scales

4. Cleveland, Museum of Fine Arts, statuette of Jonah (c.280)

Plate 31

1. Sinai, Monastery of St Catharine, icon of Christ (mid-sixth century)

2. Berlin, Museum für Spätantike und Byzantinische Kunst, icon of Abbot Abraham (from Egypt; c.600)

3. Rome, S.Sabina, wooden door, field with Christ on the cross (c.430)

Plate 32

1. Berlin, Museum für Spätantike und Byzantinische Kunst, earthenware plate with depictions of Jonah (second half of fourth century)

2. Trier, Rheinisches Landesmuseum, glass with Abraham and Jacob (fourth century)

3. Vatican Museums, glass with gold inlay (second half of fourth century)

4. Munich, Staatliche Münzsammlung, medallion of Constantine the Great (minted 315)

only makes sense if numerous churches had been decorated with such wall paintings. However, nothing has survived in Spain from so early a period. We do not know whether the large buildings which Constantine the Great founded in Rome, Constantinople, Jerusalem, Bethlehem and elsewhere had paintings, but we may assume that some did. Very scant remains are known in e.g. Demetrias (northern Greece) or Stobi (south of Skopje). Wall paintings appear in Al-Bagawat (fifth century) and Bawit (sixth century) in Egypt. S.Maria Antiqua in Rome (several layers, probably from the sixth century) and also the wall mosaics in some elaborate buildings (e.g. S.Costanza in Rome, c.350) indicate that we may assume that the walls and apses of many churches in the early period were decorated with paintings.

40. Dura Europos, baptistery of the house church: wall paintings with miracles of Christ (c.232/233), cf. pl.1.1

A larger number of paintings have been preserved in tombs. In wide areas of the empire it was customary to decorate them with figured or decorative paintings. The tradition in Rome is particularly good. Numerous wall paintings have been preserved in the tomb chambers of the catacombs and in hypogea. They begin around 200, increase in the later third century and extend to the later fourth century. A few original paintings were done in the fifth and sixth centuries. A precise dating of the various paintings is difficult, as external evidence is lacking and often the quality is not very good. A geometrical, completely unspatial system of fine lines is characteristic of decorations of the third and early fourth century (pl.18.1, Catacombs of SS.Marcellino e Pietro). Flowers, tendrils, thin garlands, vessels, masks, animals and figures or small groups of figures are interspersed. There are banquets, praying figures, shepherds, 'good shepherds', and then increasingly scenes from the Old Testament (Jonah, Daniel among the lions, the three young men in the fiery furnace, Abraham and Isaac) and the New Testament (the raising of Lazarus, etc.), of a similar kind to those which also occur on sarcophagi. In the latest, well-preserved catacombs (Via Latina or Via Dino Compagni, third quarter of the fourth century), among other things there are large scenes with many figures which are predominantly taken from the Old Testament and sometimes from the New Testament and the world of Greek sagas (pl.18.2). These paintings also indicate that we should reckon with comparable decorations in churches. In this connection a tomb in Verona which has large-scale scenes from the Old Testament and the New Testament is important (early fifth century?).

Some monuments outside Rome might be mentioned. In the Catacomb of S.Gennaro in Naples there are various paintings from the fifth/sixth century, a time when burials in Rome no longer took place in catacombs. Remains from a tomb in Alexandria will date from before Constantine; their amazingly lively style is striking. A tomb at Nicaea (Iznik, north-west Turkey, perhaps fifth century) has been preserved in particularly good condition. Several small tomb chambers have been found in Thessaloniki (fourth century); they have decorative and figured paintings (e.g. Susanna, Daniel among the lions).

Attention should be drawn to two complexes from the very few secular wall paintings which have been preserved. In Trier, splendid paintings were found under the cathedral in a banqueting hall of the imperial palace; those from the ceiling could largely be put together and are splendid examples of the art of the early fourth century. The private houses in Ephesus come from the earlier imperial period, but some rooms were renovated up to the fifth century, sometimes with pictures in the old tradition. So they give a vivid insight into homes in late antiquity.

2. Wall mosaics (tesselated mosaics)

A relatively large number of wall and ceiling mosaics have come down to us from the early Christian period. There are only a few forerunners of these in the imperial period, predominantly in fountains of various sizes. The cubes (*tesserae*) have a roughly square cross section (0.5–1 cm thick and about 2 cm long); smaller cubes and other formats were used e.g. in faces. The cubes were pressed as close together as possible in a bed of mortar which as a rule consisted of several layers. A preliminary drawing was made on the last layer before the mosaics were attached; in some cases this has still survived or has been found in restoration work. The mosaic cubes consist of stones of different colours and of glass – above all in the case of red, blue and green. One 'invention' of late antiquity was the fusing of gold leaf into glass, producing gold mosaic cubes. These were used in particular for the background, so that the scenes took on a supernatural splendour.

Precious remains of mosaics with a gold background in a small 'tomb of the Julians' (tomb M, pl.19.1) under St Peter's in Rome probably come from the time before Constantine; the tomb must have been built before 319 CE, the probable date for the beginning of St Peter's, perhaps around 300. In the rich vine pattern at the highest point of the ceiling a divine figure with a halo riding to heaven on a chariot drawn by horses has been preserved. Other scenes on the walls, above all Jonah being thrown from the ship, suggest the figure of Christ. So this is a picture of Christ in the pagan tradition, for which the iconography of Sol Invictus (the invincible sun god) has been taken over. There are parallels to the subject in paintings in catacombs.

There are various indications that there were mosaics in the apses of the churches in Rome founded by Constantine the Great, but none has survived. These will have been representative scenes like

Christ teaching between apostles or the handing down of the law (*traditio legis*) to Peter and Paul. We do not know whether the walls of the aisles were decorated with mosaics. The earliest extant mosaics appear in the mausoleum of Constantine's daughter, Constantina, today S.Constanza (c.350 CE). Pictures which have been adapted from floor mosaics appear on the ceilings of the ambulatory. The two small apses in the north and south depict figured scenes which were hardly developed for the mausoleum but reflect the apse programmes of large buildings (pl.19.3). The decoration of the central room with the cupola has been lost (but is attested by old drawings). It should be noted that white marble cubes were used for the background.

Another important monument is in Centcelles (near Tarragona, middle of the fourth century), but many questions about it are still open. The building seems to have begun as a villa, but it was not finished. The cupola of a round chamber was decorated with rich mosaics in three zones, including an extended hunting scene, scenes from the Old and New Testaments. and representative pictures. As there was a crypt, the room was probably meant to serve as a mausoleum. However, whether it was intended for the emperor Constans, son of Constantine the Great, who was murdered in the Pyrenees in 350 CE, is uncertain.

The earliest extant large apse picture is in S.Pudenziana in Rome (c.400 CE, pl.21.1). Granted, it has been cut and patched up later, but what has survived shows a grandiose composition of outstanding quality. Christ teaching, the apostles and two female figures, the embodiments of the Gentile and Jewish churches, and the four apocalyptic beings in heaven are depicted in quite a lively way, and the buildings of the heavenly Jerusalem are also characterized well. The exquisite work has no parallel in other contemporary paintings or mosaics, and even the marble work in Rome is in a different style. Only ivory and silver pieces from the time of Theodosius show a similar quality.

The mosaic of a small apse in S.Aquilino in Milan, an annexe of S.Lorenzo (third quarter of the fourth century?), similarly shows Christ teaching between apostles, but the execution is very much simpler, and the distance from S.Pudenziana considerable. In other churches from the period around 400 CE the cross will probably have been given great emphasis in the apse, along with Christ and the apostles, symbolized as lambs, as we can infer from old descriptions (basilicas in Nola and Fundi). Extensive remains of mosaics have been preserved in the baptistery of Naples cathedral (c.400 CE). They show rich ornamentation and scenes which have been taken over from large compositions, e.g. the handing down of the law and the four apocalyptic creatures.

S.Maria Maggiore in Rome was restored after a fire in 432–440 CE and decorated with a cycle of mosaics which has been largely preserved on the walls of the nave and the triumphal arch. The present apse comes from the thirteenth century; the mosaics glorify Mary; there are representative scenes from the childhood of Christ on the triumphal arch. Mary, who had been acknowledged 'Mother of God' at the Council of Ephesus in 431, is prominent. Events from the Old Testament are depicted in lively scenes in the nave. In the apse, for the first time in the early Christian period, there is a representation of Mary enthroned with her child, and martyrs, perhaps with a rich vine pattern as a background. The antechamber to the Lateran baptistery in Rome (decorated in 432–440) can give an impression of this. On the basis of the extant parts of S.Sabina in Rome (422–432), the west wall can be supplied with a large inscription which has even been handed down in written sources. The mosaics in the nave of S.Sabina are lost, and only the panel mosaics over the arcades have survived. Very scant remains have been found in the apse which show that the painting existing today (done by T.Zuccari in around 1560) has adopted the theme of the early Christian period, including Christ teaching between apostles; however, all the details have been altered in the style of the time.

After a gap, there follows in Rome the splendid apse mosaic of SS.Cosma e Damiano (526–530). It introduces a new feature, namely a concentration on a few large figures, with Christ dominant in the centre; alongside him are Peter and Paul with the titular saints, St Theodore and the founder, Pope Felix IV. The later mosaics are not so artistically executed, and copy and simplify earlier models in different ways (e.g.S.Lorenzo, 579–590; S.Agnese, 625–638; S.Stefano Rotondo, c.650).

The remains of mosaics have been preserved in several other places in Italy; these show that originally a great many churches, even small buildings in remote places, had precious decorations. Mention might be made of baptisteries in Albenga (late fifth century) and Casaranello (sixth century); chapels of martyrs in Vicenza (middle of fifth century), Milan (S.Vittore by Lorenzo, late fifth century) and S.Maria Capua Vetere (fifth century), along with the Catacomb of S.Gennaro in Naples (middle of the fifth century).

A unique treasure of early Christian and early Byzantine mosaics has been preserved in Ravenna. The city was of no importance in the Middle Ages and modern times, so the old churches were neither pulled down and replaced with new ones nor heavily restored – e.g. in the baroque period. The series of mosaics begins with the Mausoleum of Galla Placidia (c.450), which is particularly impressive with its largely preserved decoration of quite outstanding quality. There follow the baptisteries of the Orthodox (c.458) and the Arians (c.500) and the Archepiscopal Chapel (c.500). Only the basilica S.Apollinare Nuovo (beginning of the sixth century, some alterations after 561, pls. 3.2, 20.1) give some idea of a large interior richly decorated with mosaics, even if the original apse is lost and the level of the floor has been raised considerably. In three zones the pictures are in tiers, one above another; at the very top, under the ceiling, is an extensive New Testament cycle, the first extant one of its kind. Sometimes stronger Byzantine influence is expressed in the mosaics of S.Vitale (c.540/550), which are limited to the sanctuary. The two pictures of the empress Theodora and the emperor Justinian are worth noting; they give some idea of the splendour of the court. The apse mosaic of S.Michele in Africisco (c.545), now in Berlin, is in a very bad state of preservation. The end of the Ravenna mosaics is marked by the apse of S.Apollinare in Classe (c.549), with an unusual and impressive transfiguration of Christ on Mount Tabor.

In the East of the Empire the tradition is very much worse than in the West. The mosaics and paintings of the early Christian and early Byzantine period were largely destroyed in the iconoclastic dispute (730–843). However, the remains show that at one time there were numerous mosaics. The extant examples are distributed over a wide area. They do not allow us to develop a stylistic and thus chronological sequence, so it is very difficult to put any of the mosaics in chronological order. In the Acheiropoeitos in Thessaloniki, splendid ornamental remains on the underside of the arches show that the church was once richly decorated with mosaics (third quarter of fifth century). The fantastic architecture in the lower area of the cupola of Hagios Georgios in Thessaloniki, into which saints have been inserted, is extraordinary (probably c.500, pl.20.2). Decorations of the kind that appear on the wall paintings of Pompeii from the earlier first century CE have been taken over and transformed here. A great vision of Christ was depicted in the cupola of Hagios Georgios, but only a few remains and preliminary drawings have been preserved. The original openings on to the ambulatory show rich ornamental decoration in the barrel vaultings. The subjects and the quality of the mosaics in the cupola of Hagios Georgios are extraordinary. There are no parallels, so that the decoration has been dated to very different times. Perhaps it was executed around 500 CE. The small, severely mutilated church of Hosios David in Thessaloniki has one special feature in the apse, a well-preserved mosaic which shows the vision of Ezekiel with the enthroned Christ (c.500). The representation will not have been designed for this church but for a large building, not known to us, and in all probability its apse.

There is no evidence of cycles of scenes from the Old Testament and New Testament on the walls of naves in the Eastern empire, as there is in Rome and Ravenna. We may perhaps presuppose that they formed part of imperial foundations in the capital Constantinople and other prominent buildings, but all have been destroyed. In the provinces there do not seem to have been patrons for such expensive projects. That can be seen very well in Hagios Demetrios in Thessaloniki, a famous pilgrimage church which was built in the late fifth century and renovated and rebuilt in the seventh. Despite many destructions, the latest when the city was burned in 1917, a number of mosaics have survived. These are individual donations, i.e. 'fixed icons', which probably extend from the fifth century into the Middle Ages.

Some mosaics have been preserved from the early Byzantine period which must help to fill the large gaps in the earlier tradition to some extent. There is a monumental Transfiguration of Christ in the apse of the monastery of St Catharine on Sinai (between 548 and 565). S.Apollinare in Classe in Ravenna (c.549) and, with another theme, Hosios David in Thessaloniki are comparable. In Lythran-komi on Cyprus (c.530) and in Porec (c.550), Mary and the child are enthroned in the centre of the apse, a representation which can be inferred for S.Maria Maggiore in Rome (432–440). The mosaic in the church of Kiti (Cyprus) was probably made in the early seventh century; this shows the Mother of God standing between the archangels. Also from the seventh century is the first extant picture from the cycle of festivals which is not in an apse, a representation of Christ in the temple; it was found in the Kalenderhane Cami in Istanbul, but its original context is unknown (it is now in the Archaeological Museum).

Rich decorative mosaics have been preserved in Hagia Sophia, Constantinople (Istanbul), which at least in part come from the time of the building of the church (532–537) and subsequent years. An enthroned Mother of God and in the cupola Christ as Pantocrator will probably already have been depicted in the apse under Justinian. However, these and other mosaic figures were destroyed in the iconoclastic dispute.

When we admire mosaics of the early Christian period, we must remember that earlier, far more churches were decorated with them, some even in remote places. Sometimes very scant remains have been preserved, sometimes mosaic stones have been found in the rubble; more often we just have references in ancient literature. Examples are the church in Abu Mina in Egypt with a very small fragment (early sixth century), a village church in southern Asia Minor (c.500), the cathedral in Trier (late fourth-century phase) with its scant remains, and St Gereon in Cologne (late fourth century), which is mentioned in ancient literature.

After the iconoclastic dispute some important churches in the Byzantine empire were given mosaics of excellent quality, both in the capital Constantinople and in several buildings in the province (e.g. Hagia Sophia in Thessaloniki, Hosios Lukas, Nea Mone on Chios, Daphni, Paregoritissa in Arta). In the West the tradition begins e.g. in the Norman churches on Sicily (Cefalù, Palermo, Martorana and Palatina; Monreale), in St Mark's Venice, in the baptistery of Florence, in Pisa cathedral and in a number of churches in Rome, and also in the Carolingian decoration of the Palatine Chapel in Aix (c.800).

3. Wall coverings in panel mosaics

Panel mosaics (*opus sectile*, 'cut work') were sometimes already used for covering walls in the time of the Roman empire and then in the early Christian period. The material used was precious kinds of marble and porphyry of various colours, and for walls also coloured glass panels, which were cut into different forms. Geometrical and floral patterns and figures were composed with them.

The 'basilica' which Junius Bassus, consul in 331 CE, had built in Rome had very splendid decorations. Various kinds of figured fields were inserted into rich zones of ornament (it has been destroyed; old drawings and four figured fields have been preserved). The basilica in Trier (beginning of the fourth century) also had wall coverings made from panel mosaics, but these can now only be reconstructed sketchily.

An unusual find came to light in Cenchreae, the harbour of Corinth on the Saronic Gulf (it is now in the Isthmian museum in Corinth), of more than 100 panels (with a surface area of over 150 square metres) consisting of glass panel mosaics. They probably come from Egypt. They were put aside in a room and were probably lost in an earthquake and a lowering of the coast in 375 CE. Pairs of panels were made facing each other and put into wooden frames. Parts of various decorative and figured representations, including impressive landscapes with large complexes of villas by the sea and high fields with human figures, e.g. Homer and Plato, have survived. For what building this precious decoration was destined is unknown.

In Ostia an expensively decorated room has been uncovered outside the Porta Marina in a large house complex; its purpose is unclear (c.11 m x 8 m floor area). The walls, more than 7 metres high, were decorated on the sides with splendid panel mosaics made of various kinds of stones (dated by coin finds to the end of the fourth century). These have geometrical and floral patterns and large scenes with lions tearing animals apart. In the middle is a small field with a bust of Christ which hangs on the wall like an icon (pl.22.1).

There is no indication that the room had a sacral function, and it may have served profane purposes.

A wall-covering in marble panel mosaic is attested in numerous early Christian churches and baptisteries. Examples are S.Costanza (c.350), the entry hall of the baptistery of the Salvator Church (S.Giovanni in Laterano, second quarter of the fifth century), and S.Sabina (c.430) in Rome, S.Ambrogio in Milan (late fourth century), the cathedral in Trier (late fourth century phase?) and Hagios Demetrios in Thessaloniki (late fifth century). This is predominantly a geometrical pattern, but sometimes it is also a rich floral pattern; occasionally animals are depicted.

A fragment of glass panel (second half of the fourth century) shows the head of the apostle Thomas between a tondo with cross and a column; this therefore comes from a larger context (now in Corning). It was probably made in Egypt, perhaps at the same time and in the same workshop as the panels from Cenchreae. Whether it belonged to a (church?) decoration there or was already exported in late antiquity must remain open.

Wall coverings of panel mosaic can also be found from the early Byzantine period (e.g. in Hagia Sophia, Istanbul, 532/537) and in the Middle Ages (e.g. in Hosios Lukas, early eleventh century). They were imitated in paintings both in the early Christian period and later, in an attempt to give the impression of valuable wall decoration when the costly stone or glass material was too expensive.

4. Floors with tesselated and panel mosaics

In houses, villas, palaces, public buildings and churches the floors consisted of various kinds of material. A composition floor or one of clay blocks was the simplest. Large marble slabs were evidently thought valuable. Hagia Sophia in Istanbul (532–537) and the Acheiropoeitos in Thessaloniki (second half of the fifth century) are examples of buildings which had them. Large limestone slabs were a cheaper substitute and can be found in various places. The very expensive panel mosaics (*intarsia*, *opus sectile*) and the considerably cheaper tesselated mosaics (mosaics from small *tesserae*) are numerous. In Rome in the early period panel mosaics were evidently the rule and tesselated mosaics the exception. By contrast, in the Balkans, in Asia Minor, Syria and Palestine, Arabia, North Africa and probably Spain the mosaics are predominantly tesselated, and panel mosaics are rare. Examples of panel mosaics in the more remote areas of the empire are the 'basilica' (early fourth century) and the cathedral (late fourth-century phase) in Trier, the octagon in the palace of Thessaloniki (early fourth century), the octagon in Philippi (sixth-century phase) and the church in Qalat Siman, Syria (first half of sixth-century phase).

Panel mosaics. Valuable pieces of marble of different colours were used, cut into geometrical patterns. Very varied ornamental decorations were executed in it (pl.22.2). The material was imported into the Mediterranean area from various quarries. Red and grey granite was particularly expensive, as was above all porphyry from Egypt and a green marble from Laconia. The panel mosaic stands in a rich tradition from the time of the empire. There are forerunners from the second century BCE onwards. It seems to have been so popular in Rome in the early Christian period that earlier marble panels from abandoned Roman buildings could be taken out and used again.

Panel mosaics occur throughout the early Christian and early Byzantine period. They spread widely in the Middle Ages – in the early Christian tradition – both in Byzantine churches and in Rome and other places in Italy, and also in Germany. Thus parts of the floors of the Palatine Chapel in Aachen were made from older buildings in Ravenna. In Cologne in the Middle Ages panels from earlier Roman buildings seem to have been reused in different churches.

Tesselated mosaics. From the Hellenistic period floors were decorated with these mosaics. Their forerunners are the expensive and rare flint mosaics (e.g. in Pella, Sikyon, Olynthus in Greece). During the time of the empire there were numerous tesselated mosaics in all parts of the empire. In the early Christian period they were similarly widespread, both in churches and baptisteries and in palaces, villas and prominent private houses. Panel mosaics predominated merely in Rome.

The individual stones (Latin *tesserae*) are usually bigger in the floor mosaics than in the wall mosaics (around 1 cm by 2 cm). The cubes were pressed close together in a mortar bed, and the surface was smoothed as far as possible. Different stones were used, and also brick for red colouring. Glass pieces, which are used regularly in wall mosaics for certain blue, green and red colours, are very rare in floors, as they are too fragile.

In the churches there are three possibilities for subjects, which cannot always be precisely divided and which can also overlap: 1. the motives are only geometrical or floral, and no human beings or animals are depicted; 2. small fields are made with borders or vine patterns, rectangular or rounded, into which animals or human figures are inserted; 3. there are fields of different sizes with smaller or larger figured scenes (pl.23). In some churches we can see how the mosaics were not planned as an integral floor surface. Rather, individual parts were given by different patrons; these surfaces often differed in decoration, subjects and style. Often the patrons had an inscription introduced into the mosaic, in which they were named. Only rarely is a date for the making of the mosaic given.

There is a wide range of geometrical and floral decorations, and also of representations of animals. Various personifications appear as figures, including the four seasons, the twelve months or the four rivers of paradise. In the larger fields, peacocks or deer in a frame can be seen (cf. Ps.42; pl.23.1); hunts or bucolic landscapes with shepherds and their animals (pl.23.2), and often Orpheus among the animals, are depicted. One exception is the map of the Holy Land in the famous Madaba mosaic in Jordan (middle of the sixth century), which took up a large part of the church and showed pilgrims the holy places, with Jerusalem at the centre.

Figures from the biblical stories or scenes from the Old or New Testaments are very rare, and a picture of Christ (in Hinton, England, pl.19.2) seems a complete exception. Evidently there was a reluctance to tread on such depictions. The few examples include mosaics in Aquileia and in Israel which depict Jonah, and two in Syria which show Adam. However, there are often representations of crosses.

In palaces and houses there are decorations and figures similar to those in churches, and pictures from the world of the Greek sagas and from daily life. Examples are the villa of Piazza Armerina, Sicily (first half of the fourth century), splendid houses in Paphos on Cyprus (fourth century), a villa in Argos (Greek, sixth century), villas in Daphne near Antioch (from different periods), or the peristyle in the imperial palace of Constantinople (sixth century?).

We do not know whether churches from the time before Constantine had already been decorated with floor mosaics. The earliest extant example could be the double church which Bishop Theodore had built in Aquileia (313–319). The mosaics portray, among other subjects, the story of Jonah. However, perhaps the inscription of the bishop and the Christian scenes have been inserted into an earlier pagan mosaic. The church in El Asnam (Algeria), the mosaics of which have no figures, has been dated to 324 BCE. There are a few other examples from the fourth century, including St Gereon in Cologne (very scant remains); numerous tesselated mosaics have been preserved from the fifth century, and they were very popular indeed in the sixth century.

In the Middle Ages in the Byzantine empire, tesselated mosaics with figures are usually to be found on the floor; one of the very few exceptions is the church in Mesopotam (southern Albania, late thirteenth century). There are tesselated mosaics in a number of churches in Italy (e.g. in Otranto, 1163–1165; Pomposa, c.1206). The Old Testament subjects and the zodiac in St Gereon, Cologne (1151–1156), are quite unusual; they are among the last offshoots of the early Christian tesselated mosaics.

5. Mosaics as tombstones

In a very few areas of the Roman empire, mosaics were used as tombstones on the floors of churches and other buildings. A large number can be found in western North Africa (above all in Tunisia, and some also in Algeria) and fewer in Spain, in individual instances in Sicily, Grado and Homs (Syria). Pagan precursors are known from North Africa, Salona (Dalmatia) and Ostia. So Christians take up an earlier tradition.

The tombstone mosaics have vine patterns, animals, crosses and inscriptions, usually in a frame, and more rarely one or more figures; exceptionally, there is a hunting scene. The individual examples can be dated only approximately. The group begins in the late fourth century, has its heyday in the fifth century, and runs into the fifth century with some pieces which decline markedly in quality. A very much later, medieval, example which seems to stand in the old tradition is the tombstone of Abbot Gilbert in Maria Laach, who died in 1152; this has a half-portrait of the abbot and an inscription (now in Bonn).

6. Panel paintings and icons

There will have already been a large number of panel paintings in Greek and Roman times. As they were made of wood, almost all of them have been lost. A very fine example preserved by chance shows the emperor Septimius Severus with his consort and children (from Egypt, in Berlin, c.200 CE). This will not have been an individual picture but will be one of a large group of pictures of the emperor spread all over the Roman empire. Only in one area, in Fayum, Egypt, have numerous panel paintings, the 'mummy portraits', been preserved because of the favourable climatic conditions and special burial customs. They show portraits of men and women, more rarely also of children, and, as can often be seen, were later used for mummies. The series extends from the early first century to the fourth century CE. Christianity evidently brought about a change in burial customs, and at a later date mummies were no longer made.

Isolated panel paintings have also been preserved from Egypt. In addition to the picture of Septimius Severus and his family, a triptych (three-panelled 'folding altarpiece') with busts of a man – probably dead – and the gods Serapis and Isis on the wings is particularly important (middle of the third century, in Malibu).

Two different painting techniques were customary for the pictures, namely tempera painting (with egg to bind the colours) and the technically very expensive wax painting or 'encaustic' material (with beeswax as a binding agent).

At an early stage – very much in the pagan tradition – Christians seem to have made panel paintings of the biblical persons who were very important for them, i.e. of Christ, Mary, apostles, etc., and perhaps also pictures of bishops. However, this can only be inferred from references; none has survived.

The 'official' church opposed the panel painting – and the wall painting. However, popular piety called for pictures, so there probably will also have been panel pictures from the third century on. They quite certainly existed in the late fourth century. The painted bust of Christ in the Catacomb of Commodilla in Rome or the picture made of a panel mosaic in Ostia hung up like an icon (both late fourth century), which are framed like independent pictures, give some idea of them.

The transition from the panel picture to the venerated icon (from the Greek *eikon*, image), which must be a faithful copy of the original and is typical of the Eastern church, appears to have taken place slowly in the course of the sixth and seventh centuries; it culminated in the Orthodox doctrine of icons, which governed Orthodox Christians from the end of the iconoclastic dispute in 843. The earliest icons to have survived come from the early Byzantine period and as a result of favourable political and climatic conditions have been preserved in St Catherine's Monastery on Sinai and in places in Egypt. There are also some examples in Rome, but they are mostly very fragmented and later were largely painted over. There are both tempera and wax paintings and predominantly representations of Christ (pl.31.1), Mary and saints, but there is also a picture of an abbot (in Berlin, pl.31.2).

Panel paintings become highly significant in the Western empire from the Middle Ages on, as did icons in the Eastern church after the iconoclastic dispute; they are extremely important groups of pictorial art.

7. The illustration of books

In Greek and Roman times, books took the form of a scroll (*rotulus*). The text, written in ink and by hand, was put in parallel columns. The scroll, which was between 9 and 10 metres long, was unrolled with the left hand and rolled up with the left hand while it was being read. The material used was parchment (the hides of small and young animals, especially sheep, goats, calves and asses, which had been given special treatment, named after the city of Pergamum in Asia Minor). After the late fourth century BCE, the much cheaper papyrus was used (derived from the papyrus reeds which grow in Egypt). More expensive manuscripts had figures or small scenes, called 'miniatures' (from Latin *minium*, a particular colour of red), inserted. The Jews also used the *rotulus* for their sacred scriptures (Torah scrolls).

In the first century CE the form of the 'codex' (from Latin *codex* or *caudex*, 'volume', 'notebook') appeared; this predominated from the fourth century and corresponds to our present-day books. It was preferred by Christians, possibly in order to distinguish their Holy Scripture from the Jewish Torah scroll even in form.

The main material used for codices was parchment. Of course not all the Old Testament and the New Testament could be contained in a hand-written codex with miniatures, nor even all the books of the Old Testament. Different divisions were used, e.g. manuscripts with Genesis, the Pentateuch (the first five books of the OT), the Octateuch (the first eight books of the OT) or the Gospels (Evangeliar).

When Christian manuscripts decorated with book painting begin, whether we are to presuppose Jewish illustrated manuscripts, and what their relation to the Christian illustrations was, are all open questions. The earliest extant example is some pages of the Old Latin translation of the Bible which were found in Quedlinburg, the Quedlinburg Itala (early fifth century, most of it in Berlin). But there are various indications that Christians already had illustrated manuscripts very much earlier, probably from the third century on. This can be inferred, for example, from the wall paintings in the synagogue and the house church of Dura Europos. As a series of scenes has been depicted in a similar way in other areas at a much later time, it seems likely that we should presuppose biblical manuscripts as models for the wall paintings. They must have been earlier than the wall paintings. Two examples from the years 200/220 could have come into the remote city in the east of Syria and there been copied freely and in sections for the wall paintings.

An illustrated calendar of the year 354 CE was made for a Christian, but is completely within the earlier Roman tradition and contains nothing specifically Christian (preserved only in tenth-century drawings from a copy of the Carolingian period, in Paris). The Cotton Genesis was very richly decorated with large-scale figured scenes, but only fragments have been preserved: the place and time of its origin are uncertain (fifth century?, now in London). Two splendid Evangeliars and a Genesis manuscript in which the parchment has been dyed purple, and silver or gold inks have been used for the script (Vienna Genesis, Evangeliar of Rosano; some pages of an evangeliar from Sinope, in Paris), were already made in the sixth century, the early Byzantine period. Where they were made cannot be determined: it could be Constantinople or Antioch, perhaps even Jerusalem. The purple dye and the rich decoration suggest that members of the imperial family or top dignitaries will have commissioned these manuscripts. They are outstanding testimony to the artistic heyday in the time of the emperor Justinian (527–565).

A Syriac evangeliar made by a monk called Rabulla in 586 comes from northern Mesopotamia (now in Florence). It may go back to an earlier work from one of the artistic centres of the empire (Antioch? Jerusalem), and is important because of its large-scale treatment of the festivals. Other illustrated biblical manuscripts of the early Christian period can be inferred only from later copies: they include the Ashburnham Pentateuch (seventh century, Paris) and the Utrecht Psalter (830).

Some pagan manuscripts with miniatures have survived from late antiquity: the Vatican Virgil (early fifth century), which may have been produced in the same scriptorium in Rome as the Quedlinburg Itala; the Roman Virgil, of much inferior quality, possibly from a province (later fifth century, in the Vatican); the miniatures cut out of a manuscript of Homer's *Iliad*, the Ilias Ambrosiana, which was produced in the East of the empire, perhaps in Constantinople or Alexandria (late fifth century in Milan); and the Vienna Dioscurides, a splendid manuscript which was made for Princess Anicia Juliana in the early sixth century in Constantinople and above all contains large-format pictures of plants (383 of the original 435 or so pages have survived).

The relationship between text and picture is very interesting and has to be investigated specially for each manuscript. Sometimes the texts – of Holy Scripture! – are abbreviated to make room for a concentrated series of pictures; sometimes there are details in the miniatures which are not mentioned in the text and thus come from other traditions. As a rule scribe and painter will not have been identical. In extensive and well-preserved manuscripts it can be seen that several painters were at work.

All in all, only a very few examples of book painting from the early Christian period have been preserved. So far it has not been possible to establish centres of manufacture and their stylistic peculiarities, so stylistic and chronological sequences cannot be developed either. The extant manuscripts with paintings must be seen as individual items – of course very precious. Numerous manuscripts with miniatures have come down from the early and high Middle Ages; book painting was one of the most important genres of art both in the Byzantine empire and in the West. Frequently we can see that the mediaeval painters have gone back to early Christian and early Byzantine models.

V

Sculptures

There are substantially fewer sculptures from the early Christian period than from previous centuries. The early Christian sarcophagi form the largest group. However, there are considerably fewer of them than pagan sarcophagi: around 2,500 Christian examples from the third to sixth centuries compared with more than 15,000 pagan examples. The difference cannot be connected with the fact that in late antiquity the population was impoverished and no one could afford sarcophagi decorated with reliefs any longer. Rather – for reasons so far unknown – burial customs changed in large parts of the Roman empire: sarcophagi with expensive decorations had largely gone out of fashion. It is particularly striking that there are very few early Christian sarcophagi in the eastern provinces of the empire. However, e.g. hundreds, probably thousands of churches in the Balkans, in Asia Minor, Syria, Palestine and Arabia and in North Africa, many with valuable decorations, attest the economic prosperity of these areas between the fourth and the sixth centuries CE.

1. Sarcophagi

In the Roman empire it was customary in the first and early second centuries CE to cremate the dead and put the ashes in urns. In the early second century – for reasons as yet unknown to us – customs changed: there was a move towards burying the corpses. More prosperous families used sarcophagi (coffins, from the Greek *sarkophagos* and the Latin derivative *sarcophagus*), which were decorated with reliefs. They usually consisted of stone, marble for preference, and were widespread throughout the Roman empire. Centres of manufacture were Rome, Athens and Dokimeion in

Phrygia (Western Turkey); there was also local work in many of the provinces. In Athens and Dokimeion production ended around 260/270 CE; there are no Christian examples from these important workshops.

Sarcophagi with Christian themes have been preserved above all from Rome. More than 1,000 examples have survived from the period from the third century to shortly after 400 CE, but many of them are only in fragments. Ravenna was a further centre of manufacture (from the beginning of the fifth century to the sixth, with some later examples down to the eighth century), however, numbers are far fewer (around 50). After 330, sarcophagi were made in the new capital Constantinople (Istanbul), but there were very few of them (again around 50), and the craftsmanship was very different. In addition, in some provinces there were sarcophagi with Christian themes or examples which were demonstrably used by Christians; however, these are almost always individual items. Only Gaul had any great production, and that was over a longer period.

In discussing sarcophagi we shall first consider some general questions and then look at the three centres of manufacture, Rome, Ravenna and Constantinople, finally going on to consider the provinces.

(a) General questions

Forms of sarcophagi. The forms of the early Christian sarcophagi are largely in the tradition of the pagan examples. They are largely long rectangular chests. In Rome, early examples include a few with rounded corners. Occasionally the sarcophagi are not made of one large block but constructed from several pieces. Sometimes they consist of individual slabs which are held together with clamps. In Asia Minor there are examples which are worked out of the solid rock, and are thus fixed. In Rome the lids usually have the form of a flat slab; on the front there is a raised border which is decorated with reliefs and often also has a panel for the inscription. In Ravenna and the Eastern provinces the lids almost always have the form of a roof. This emphasizes the purpose of the sarcophagus as a house for the dead. Examples with rounded lids are rare (Ravenna, Asia Minor). The slabs which closed the *loculi* (burial places in catacombs) and parts of walled sarcophagi ('pseudo-sarcophagi') can be included among sarcophagi, as their decoration is connected with that of the sarcophagi.

The following forms can be distinguished:

- *Frieze sarcophagi*: these have a frieze running round them with figures or decorative motifs (diag.41.1); they are frequent in Rome (pl.24.1) and Gaul, and rare in other provinces (pl.26.1) and Constantinople; some elaborate examples have two zones one above another (Rome, perhaps Gaul, diag.41.2); in Ravenna the friezes are framed at the sides with pillars or columns ('Torre Nova group', pl.24.3).
- *Column sarcophagi*: there are relatively few of these, but they were often very elaborate. These sarcophagi have an architectural division by columns, half-columns or pillars (Rome, Ravenna, Constantinople, Gaul, diag.41.3; pl.25.2). Examples with two zones are an exception; they include the most splendid early Christian sarcophagus from Rome (of Junius Bassus, in St Peter's, pl.24.2).
- *Tree sarcophagi*: these are derived from the column sarcophagi; the figures and groups of figures are separated by trees (Rome, perhaps Gaul, diag. 41.4).
- *Fluted sarcophagi*: on the front there are smaller fields (usually three) with one or more figures or scenes with figures and between them two larger 'flutes' (concave fillets) (diag.41.5) in an S shape or running vertically; more elaborate pieces have two zones (Rome, Gaul, North Africa; diag.41.6).
- *Chest sarcophagi*: these have a raised border which runs round all the sides; in the early Christian period the form does not occur often; they have sometimes figured, but usually decorative or symbolic representations (e.g. the 'Sarcophagus of the Princes' in Istanbul, pl.25.1,3; Ravenna, Asia Minor, Syria, diag.41.7).

In many examples in the three centres and also in the provinces only the front bears reliefs; the cutting of the sides and the back is relatively crude. Sometimes there are flat reliefs on the sides, and rarely they are worked more deeply (e.g. in Ravenna). Only in exceptional cases do all four sides bear reliefs (e.g. in Ravenna; the 'Sarcophagus of the Princes' in Istanbul; the 'Milan City Gate Sarcophagus' and a few late fourth-century examples from Rome).

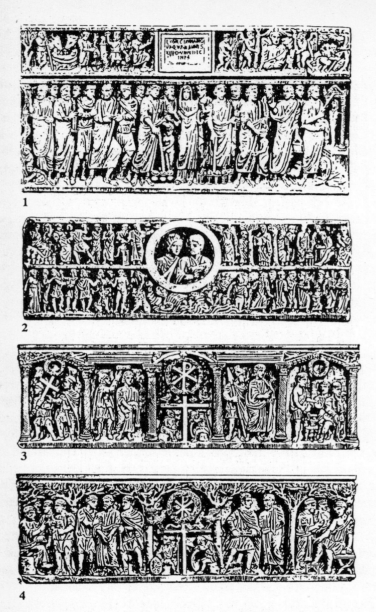

1

2

3

4

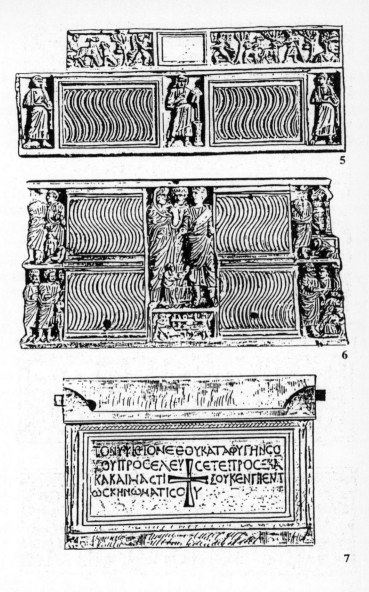

41. Forms of early Christian sarcophagi: 1. frieze sarcophagus; 2. two-zone frieze sarcophagus; 3. column sarcophagus; 4. tree sarcophagus; 5. fluted sarcophagus; 6. two-zone fluted sarcophagus; 7. chest sarcophagus.

The reuse of pagan sarcophagi. Quite often we can see that new sarcophagi were not made for Christian clients, but older pagan sarcophagi were reused. Sometimes a cross was worked out of part of the representation; often the sarcophagus was 'Christianized' simply by the carving of one or more crosses along with an inscription. The examples are widely scattered over the Roman empire. In Rome, Christian scenes have been subsequently worked on the sides of two examples and in some others covers with Christian designs were put on 'neutral' chests which had been made for stock.

Sarcophagi with 'neutral' themes. Various sarcophagi with subjects which are neither clearly pagan nor clearly Christian pose a problem; these are above all sarcophagi with pastoral scenes ('bucolic' sarcophagi), or one or two 'good shepherds' with 'philosophers' and praying figures. They begin around 250/260 and continue to the early fourth century CE; one piece comes from the end of the fourth century. Usually these are called 'neutral' sarcophagi, as they could be used both by adherents of the pagan religions and by Christians.

Sarcophagi from the early Christian period with pagan themes. All examples with clearly 'pagan' themes disappear in Rome in 311/313 CE with the edicts of Constantine. For example, not a single sarcophagus with Greek myths or with scenes from the Dionysian cycle can be dated after 313. However, the representations on some later sarcophagi, e.g. embodiments of the four seasons, with wine-treading and above all with hunting scenes, stand in the earlier tradition. They may have been used by prosperous 'pagans' but also by Christians, as we can see e.g. in the case of the hunting sarcophagi (e.g. in Osimo and Rome, Cimitero Maggiore). The hunting sarcophagi end in Rome around 370/380 CE. The latest example with a subject which is not clearly Christian is a vintage scene with shepherds in the Vatican (end of the fourth century).

Materials from which the sarcophagi were made. The materials are of different kinds. The more expensive sarcophagi are almost all made of marble. In Rome it had to be imported, mostly from Luni (Carrara, in north–west Italy) or from Proconessus, the island of marble (present-day Marmara), near Constantinople (Istanbul); there are no more detailed investigations. All the Ravenna sarcophagi seem to be made of marble from Proconnesus (pl.24.3). In Constantinople, marble (from Proconessus, pl.25.1, 3) was used for only a few examples; for most a relatively bad limestone was used (pl.25.2); in addition there is marble speckled with green (from Thessaly, *verde antico*), marble which is almost black, one instance of marble speckled with red, stones which look like alabaster, and other examples.

In the provincial sarcophagi, above all local marble (pl.26.2), limestone, sandstone (pl.26.1) or volcanic rock (pl.26.3) have been used. Exceptions are made of precious porphyry (porphyrites), which occurs only in Egypt and was used for imperial burials in Rome and Constantinople; lead, from which a few Christian sarcophagi in Syria (diag.43) and other isolated examples were cast; painted wood in Egypt; and, in one example in which St Paulinus was buried in Trier, wood with metal studs.

Technique of manufacture. Only in Rome have so many sarcophagi been preserved that we can say something about the technique of their manufacture. At least in the time of Constantine they seem to have been mass-produced in a strictly-organized workshop. The preparation was divided into several processes which were undertaken by sculptors trained in different ways. The use of the chisel alternates on the same piece with the use of the drill, with which greater depths could be reached quickly. Often the last processes were left out for reasons of time, and the sarcophagi were used in an 'unfinished state'. In a great many examples we can see different states of finish on a sarcophagus: more progress had been made in one part than in another. The pieces were used nevertheless, probably because a sarcophagus was urgently needed for a burial.

It has been calculated that because of the rationalized organization and the use of several craftsmen simultaneously, only seven to eight working days were needed to make a one-zone frieze sarcophagus in the time of Constantine; however, this figure seems to me to be far too low, and the conjectures need to be tested.

A *loculus* slab from Rome (now in Urbino) shows very vividly the manufacture of a sarcophagus (diag.42; pl.27.2). Eutropos, a Christian, is working on a lion's head with a drill; this is a fluted sarcophagus with two lions' heads, a form which was very popular in the later third century.

42. Grave slab of the sculptor Eutropos (section): making a sarcophagus (c.300), cf. pl.27.2.

Painted sarcophagi. The sarcophagi in Rome, Ravenna, Constantinople and probably also most of the provinces were painted. It is not easy for us to imagine what they once looked like, since remnants, usually only very small, remain of only a few examples. We will have to think in terms of relatively bright colours; in addition the ridges are often picked out with gold. Eyebrows, pupils, lips and hair were emphasized. The 'polychrome fragments' (Rome, MNR), a *loculus* slab (Rome, Catacomb Via Anapo) or a pagan sarcophagus in Trier can give some idea of what the colours once looked like.

Commissioned or made for stock. We can conjecture that one set of sarcophagi in the workshops was made for stock and then sold when needed, and others were made to special order. In Rome, the more simple examples like the fluted sarcophagi or the more modest frieze sarcophagi of the time of Constantine period may have been made for stock. This could be indicated by the fact that occasionally on figures which were to be given portrait heads (pl.24.1, lid), the head has been left as a crude mass in an unworked state (as a boss); individual work for the purchaser has not been done – for reasons unknown to us.

By contrast, in other examples there is some indication that the person commissioning the sarcophagus expressed certain wishes, in other words that the sarcophagus was made specially for him. This group may include the pre-Constantinian sarcophagi, some of the Constantinian frieze sarcophagi with an unusual sequence of figures, and also some of the two-zone frieze sarcophagi. It certainly includes those which are completely outside the framework, like the sarcophagus of Junius Bassus (pl.24.2) or the 'Milan City Gate Sarcophagus'. The sarcophagi in Ravenna and in Constantinople were probably all made to special commission, as far as can be inferred from the different subjects. In the provinces, pieces were usually individual, so we are not to assume that any were made for stock; exceptions are the fluted sarcophagus from Carthage (fifth century) and the late examples from Brac (Dalmatia).

The installation of sarcophagi. Very little is known of the original use of the early Christian sarcophagi. In Rome some were in tomb buildings. Other examples were put in catacombs. The imperial mausoleums of the Tor Pignattara and S.Costanza (pl.4), each of which contained a porphyry sarcophagus, are exceptions. Not a single one of the sarcophagi in Ravenna has been preserved in its original position. However, several of the 'pseudo-sarcophagi' in Constantinople have been found in their tomb-chambers.

We have some knowledge in the case of the provincial pieces from Asia Minor and Syria; some are in the open air, and they sometimes line the streets, but more often they are in tomb structures. Few of these have been found in the west of the empire (Spain, Arles, Trier).

The basis of a chronology. Four points may help in the chronological ordering of sarcophagi, but the presence of all four of them is an ideal: the iconography of the representation as a whole or individual groups of figures; links with a workshop; portraits or inscriptions; and style. In reality, however, considering the overall number of sarcophagi, points of contact for dates are very few.

In Rome, the sarcophagi of the time before Constantine can be connected with pagan examples for the chronological order of which we have better evidence, and thus dated. The Constantinian friezes of the arch of Constantine, together with the historical events, provide points of reference for the years after 313 CE (pl.24.1). On the basis of an inscription, three sarcophagi including one depicting a hunt are to be put around 330; they were found in Arles but come from Rome. Then the sarcophagus of Junius Bassus is a fixed point of chronology (dated to 359 by the inscription, pl.24.2). From the later years – in addition to tiny fragments which do not tells us much – dated examples from 360, 366, 392 and probably 408 CE have survived. But all four are of very modest quality, so that they do not provide any tenable basis for chronology. Sarcophagi in Tolentino and Ancona and from the Anician Mausoleum in Rome can be put in the late fourth century CE on the basis of inscriptions. As a consequence of the economic and political decline of the city and its conquest by the Goths in 410, the sarcophagi decorated with figures seem to break off in Rome soon after 400.

In Ravenna the production probably begins only after the moving of the imperial residence from Milan to Ravenna in 402 CE. There are no further points of contact, and individual pieces have to be put in a relative sequence solely on the basis of their style; thus all suggested datings are very uncertain.

For Constantinople, its inauguration as a new capital in 330 CE gives an indication of the beginning of production. But it is very difficult to place individual pieces, as none has a firm date and there are only a few other dated monuments.

Points of reference are particularly scarce for the provincial examples, so it is very difficult to give precise datings. Even if a piece can be dated by its inscription, that is of little help, as there are no other examples to connect with it. In Asia Minor three examples (332, 462 and 591/592 CE, pl.26.2) can be dated by inscriptions and also three in Syria (468/469, 486/487, 534 CE); however, they do not offer any features for comparison with other sarcophagi. The wood sarcophagus of St Paulinus in Trier (made after 358) is a special case and does not tell us anything about the sarcophagi in the Rhine–Moselle area. Some of the porphyry sarcophagi which will have been made in Alexandria can be dated on historical considerations to the second quarter of the fourth century.

So it has to be emphasized that there are considerable difficulties in establishing a chronological sequence for early Christian sarcophagi, and many of the dates proposed in the literature are only approximate.

(b) The sarcophagi in Rome

Numerous sarcophagi have been found in Rome, so that the stylistic peculiarities of the workshops in the city are well known. Some examples were exported, to northern and southern Italy, Sicily, Sardinia, Istria, Salona (Dalmatia), into Western North Africa, on the Spanish peninsula and to Gaul. The production can be traced from 270/280 to 400 CE and can be divided into various phases.

Before Constantine (from the beginning of Christian art to 311/313)

In the first and early second centuries it was customary in wide areas of the Roman empire to cremate the dead and bury the ashes in urns. There are no indications that the Christians had other customs. The earliest sarcophagus thought to have been used by a Christian is that of Prosenes (Rome, garden of the Villa Borghese). Its inscription is dated to the year 217 CE, but the formulation is not clearly Christian. Nor does anything in its decoration indicate that the dead person was a Christian; rather, it is a sarcophagus with a pagan decoration.

The first clearly Christian example is the sarcophagus of S.Maria Antiqua in Rome (c.270/280 CE). In the years before 311/313 CE a large number of sarcophagi follow (e.g. the Jonah sarcophagi, Vatican, c.290 CE; 'polychrome fragments', Rome, MNR, c.300; *loculus* seals in the Vatican and in Rome, Mus.Cap, c. 300). Lids and fragments of lids are very numerous; the chest belonging to them will have had 'neutral' depictions, and so we can no longer recognize them. Scenes from the story of Jonah predominate, but others from the Old Testament and New Testament also appear.

The sarcophagi from the pre-Constantine period in Rome have no stylistic peculiarities. As they were made to specific order in various workshops which otherwise made pagan sarcophagi, they are not uniform in either style or form of decoration or even in depictions; they are always individual items.

Constantine (c.313 to c.340)

An extensive production of sarcophagi began immediately after the edicts of Constantine; these have a completely new features, namely friezes with closely packed groups of figures and superior composition (diag.41.1). Most examples belong to the 'Peter–Christ group' which is vividly represented by the sarcophagus of Sabinus in the Vatican. In the centre a praying woman is prominent, and the sides are framed with appropriate scenes; the surfaces in between have scenes from the lives of Christ and Peter. This composition has been changed many times (pl.24.1). In addition there are just a few examples with other scenes and a series of fluted sarcophagi. Around 330 CE the two-zone frieze sarcophagi begin – in addition to the one-zone sarcophagi; most of these have a shell with the portrait of the dead person in the centre of the upper register, also overlapping on to the lower zone (diag.41.2); so too do the two-zone fluted sarcophagi (diag.41.6).

After Constantine (c.340–360/370)

In this period the number of sarcophagi declines. There are still frieze and fluted sarcophagi with one and two zones, the designs on which stand in an earlier tradition. What is new is the division with columns (diag.41.3) or trees ('tree sarcophagi', diag.41.4). Miracles of Christ continue as themes; in addition there are groups of Christ and the apostles, and above all scenes from the passion of Christ, usually with the cross as a sign of Christ's victory in the centre ('passion sarcophagi', diags.41,3,4). The most grandiose example in this phase is the sarcophagus of Junius Bassus in St Peter's, Rome, dated to 359 BCE, a two-zone column sarcophagus of outstanding quality and worthy of the prefect of the city who is buried in it: in modern terms he was the Lord Mayor of Rome, appointed by the emperor (pl.24.2). Because of the elegant figures and the excellent quality this is also referred to as the period of 'good style'.

Valentinian and Theodosius (360/370–400)

There continue to be frieze sarcophagi, column sarcophagi and also individual instances of tree sarcophagi and depictions of the passion, a group of apostles and the *traditio legis*, and also fluted sarcophagi. A new feature is a variation of the column sarcophagi with Christ teaching between the apostles; in the background they have a representation of city architecture with gates ('city-gate sarcophagus'). This forms a small closely connected group which has reliefs on all four sides and must have been produced for very distinguished people. The best known example was taken to Milan (S.Ambrogio). In this phase two further narrative scenes were created in a transformation of the column sarcophagus, first, pieces with the healing of the sick man by the pool of Bethesda and Christ's entry into Jerusalem (called both 'Bethesda sarcophagi' and 'entry sarcophagi'), and secondly the passage of the Israelites through the Red Sea ('exodus sarcophagi'). These pieces are smaller and the craftsmanship is more modest than in the case of the city-gate sarcophagi.

Later phase (after 400)

Only very few sarcophagi are known in Rome for the period after 400. Because of the economic decline of the city and the attack by the Goths in 410, production seems to have come to a standstill. There are examples with flutes which usually have a cross in the middle. Figures in the field(s) are rare. Exceptions are a chest with lattice work (in Rome, Campo Santo Teutonico) and a large well-worked fluted sarcophagus with a throne (in Frascati).

(c) The sarcophagi in Ravenna

After the imperial residence moved from Milan to Ravenna in 402 CE, independent production of sarcophagi began in the city, though the quantity was very small. The local pagan pieces had come to an end around 270. In the fourth century evidently no sarcophagi were made in Ravenna; there were only some imports from Rome. The Christian sarcophagi of the fifth century introduce completely new forms and subjects and have no points of contact with examples from the city of Rome, with the few Christian examples in northern Italy or the pagan pieces in Ravenna. Probably the sculptors came from Constantinople and brought the models for the Christian sarcophagi with them from there. Many examples in Ravenna have reliefs on all four sides, in the Eastern tradition. The rounded corners have parallels in Asia Minor, and there are also Eastern features on the edges of the roof-shaped lids.

The series begins in the early fifth century with a few examples, the friezes of which are divided by pillars or columns ('Torre Nova group', pl.24.3). A very few figures are distributed on the surfaces. On the fronts there are scenes of homage, the giving of the law and by way of exception the adoration of the three magi; on the sides there are scenes from the New Testament or the Old Testament, or apostles. In these and other examples, on the backs there are symbolic representations (lambs, deer, doves or peacocks) alongside a Christogram. Somewhat later this decoration runs on to the sides.

Perhaps rather later than the Torre Nova examples, but also still in the early fifth century, the column sarcophagi begin; these too are represented by only a few examples. The figurative sarcophagi seem to stop in the middle of the fifth century, when only decorative sarcophagi were made. Later examples are much simpler; the animals seem stunted and there is much less free room between them. There are still only animals, crosses and trees on column sarcophagi. These simpler pieces are perhaps to be dated to the time of Gothic rule, i.e. after 439. Later examples from the sixth century simplify the representations even more; the relief becomes quite flat. The last examples extend down to the eighth century.

(d) The sarcophagi in Constantinople

Constantinople was inaugurated as the new capital of the empire in 330 CE. No sarcophagi are known from the first decades; they only begin in the late fourth century. Relatively few examples have survived. For the moment it is impossible to say whether many were destroyed or whether the production was generally very small. There are figured (frieze and column) and decorative sarcophagi. The quality differs considerably; there are a few excellent pieces (of marble) and several in which the craftsmanship is very simple (from limestone). The sarcophagi had no tradition in Byzantium and Constantinople; the sculptors seem to have immigrated from the provinces, above all from Asia Minor.

A masterpiece of East Roman graphic art is the 'Sarcophagus of the Princes' (end of the fourth century, pl.25.1), which has reliefs on all four sides. It has the form of a 'chest sarcophagus' with a border which is raised on all four sides, a type popular in several groups of pagan sarcophagi of the second and third centuries in Asia Minor (above all in Bithynia and Pisidia). The 'Sarcophagus of the Princes' stands alone in this period. Column sarcophagi are represented by a few excellent fragments. The limestone fragments may have included some of sarcophagi or 'pseudo-sarcophagi' with friezes. Others show an architectural division (e.g. the examples from Taskasap, pl.25.2, and Amberliköy). The pieces are very crude, and therefore can be dated generally to the end of the fourth and the first half of the fifth century.

The decorative sarcophagi – like the figured ones – seem to begin in the late fourth century. One of the earliest examples is made of marble from Proconnesus and like the 'Sarcophagus of the Princes' belongs among the 'fluted sarcophagi' (pl.25.3). In its proportions, the form of the roof-shaped lid and the acroteria, it is very close to examples from the late second century (probably end of the fourth century). In addition there are various other decorative sarcophagi from the fifth and sixth centuries. The latest pieces (sixth/seventh centuries) are very humble and narrow, bear simple crosses as decoration, and inside show the outline of a human body with head and shoulders. The porphyry sarcophagi were probably made in Alexandria (see V,1, e).

(e) The sarcophagi in the provinces

Before Constantine

Only a very few sarcophagi can be dated to before Constantine. They include pieces in Velletri, Naples, Aire-sur-l'Adour, Berlin and London, and perhaps also Belgrade. Some lead sarcophagi from the province of Syria (probably made in Sidon, in present-day southern Lebanon) perhaps date from the time before Constantine (diag.43); their decoration is certainly very much in the pagan tradition, but the additional crosses show that they were specially commissioned for the burial of Christians. It is possible, but not certain, that the Noah sarcophagus in Trier (pl.26.1) is to be dated to the time before Constantine.

Constantine and later

Italy, Gaul. The provinces of the West were largely under the influence of Rome and there is evidence of numerous imports from Rome – as was already the case with pagan sarcophagi in the second and third centuries. There are imitations of examples from the city of Rome (above all from the fourth century) in varying numbers in Campania, northern Italy, Gaul (especially Arles) and Spain. Some examples in northern Italy and Spain seem to be dependent on the East. In Aquitania (south-west Gaul), a considerable number of sarcophagi have been preserved (more than 200 of them) which form an independent group and stand out by their predilection for varied decorations (early fifth to early sixth centuries).

Rhine-Moselle area. Most of the extant sarcophagi bear no decoration; frequently traces of chisel work remain. Only in Trier are there some examples with figures, but these have no connection with Rome, Ravenna or Gaul; they include one with Noah and his family in the ark (pl.26.1) and a second with the three young men in the fiery furnace, etc. (probably early fourth century); it is not certain whether some fragments (of the fourth century) belong to sarcophagi.

Spanish peninsula. Imports from Rome are relatively numerous. In some scattered local pieces they have been taken as a model. So far it has not proved possible to distinguish the local work clearly from that of the city of Rome. In one example (towards 400 CE), influences from Constantinople can be recognized. In the later fourth and probably first half of the fifth century various fluted sarcophagi were imported from Carthage to Tarragona (Tarraco).

Western North Africa. There have been only a few finds. Exceptionally, they follow frieze sarcophagi from the city of Rome. Fluted sarcophagi which were made in Carthage (later fourth and first half of fifth century) and in some cases exported to Tarragona (Tarraco) form a small self-contained group.

Balkans. Only a very few early Christian sarcophagi survive from the whole of the Balkans and the Aegean islands. In the second and third centuries there was a varied and sometimes very extensive production, but it breaks off almost everywhere in the second half of the third century. Only in Salona is there a small group of early

Christian sarcophagi, predominantly of limestone, exceptionally of marble. Otherwise there are only a few individual pieces (Belgrade, Dyrrachium-Durres, Ithaca, Tegea and Rhodes).

Asia Minor. A very large number of sarcophagi were made in the second and third centuries CE, and many local groups can be distinguished. The tradition breaks off in the second half of the third century. Very few sarcophagi are known from the early Christian period, almost only decorative examples. Exceptions are two column sarcophagi in Adrassus ('Rough Cilicia') with different figures (now destroyed). There are decorative pieces e.g. in Ephesus (marble garland sarcophagus of the second century reused), Arycanda (Lycia), Corycus, Adrassus (fourth/fifth century) and Alahan Monastir (chiselled from the existing rock, dated 462 CE). A marble sarcophagus in Afyon with a rounded lid is the latest extant example in Asia Minor (dated 581–592; pl.26.2).

43. Lead sarcophagus from Sidon (present-day Lebanon): lid and long side (c.300?).

Syria, Palestine. In these areas the situation is similar to that in Asia Minor. Despite the prosperity of the land in the early Christian period, which is attested e.g. by the numerous church buildings, very few sarcophagi are known, and they are only decorative, e.g. in Apameia (two dated 468/469 and 534), in El Bara (in a splendid tomb building, pl.17.2), at the citadel in Aleppo, scattered in northern Syria (diag.41.7), and in the 'central building' in Resafa (third quarter of the sixth century?). An example in Homs made of marble from Proconnesus is unusual; it has no parallels in Constantinople and so was probably made locally. Two pieces in Qanawat (southern Syria) made of basalt have somewhat richer decorative ornamentation (fifth century?; pl.26.3).

Lead sarcophagi were also produced in some places in Syria and Palestine in the early Christian period. Some of good quality come from a workshop in Sidon which made numerous pagan and also some Jewish lead sarcophagi (early fourth century, diag.43). The very few scattered other ones with Christian motives are of much lower quality than the pagan examples (fourth to sixth centuries CE).

Egypt. Hardly any sarcophagi are known. A group of painted wood sarcophagi from the early Christian period has not yet been published. The porphyry sarcophagi which have been found in Rome, Constantinople and a few other places were probably made in Alexandria. Some examples have figured reliefs. The battle sarcophagus which was found in the mausoleum of Helena (Tor Pignattara) in Rome was perhaps originally intended for the Emperor Constantine the Great. The example with cupids picking grapes stood in the mausoleum of Constantina, the daughter of Constantine (both now in the Vatican). A fragment in Istanbul also shows a vintage. A few other fragments will belong to similar sarcophagi which were intended for the imperial family of the time of Constantine; they were made around 320–340 CE, but show no kind of Christian themes. Later, simple porphyry sarcophagi were used for the burials of emperors; these are large and sometimes have crosses as decorations on the lids. It is not possible to attribute them to particular persons. Only one example, which unusually has rounded sides, seems to have been intended for the emperor Julian (died 363).

2. Other sculptures

Relatively few but very different pieces of other sculpture need to be mentioned: some 'historical reliefs', statues large and small, portraits, reliefs with Christian and pagan subjects, relief icons, tomb reliefs and doors of carved wood. To these might be added tombstones with engraved inscriptions and other representations, even if they really cannot be classed as reliefs. The Christian examples from the time before Constantine are put first, as they are particularly important for the origin of Christian pictorial art.

Before Constantine

Already at the end of the second century CE, followers of Carpocrates, i.e. members of a Gnostic sect, are said to have had not only portraits of Pythagoras, Plato and Aristotle but also a picture of Christ. It is reported of the emperor Alexander Severus (reigned 222–235 CE) that as well as pictures of Abraham, Orpheus, Apollonius of Tyana and of his family ancestors he also had a picture of Christ in his domestic sanctuary (*lararium*). It is hard to judge what we are to make of these reports, and we do not know what the pictures mentioned looked like. A heavily enlarged seated statue in the Vatican which has been worked over shows Hippolytus, 'bishop' of Rome; this is the statue of a woman from the second century CE which in 233/235 was reused for the Christian 'bishop'.

Christian sculptures can only be detected from 270/280 CE, e.g. in a group of excellent small figures which were perhaps put in a tomb (now in Cleveland, pl.30.4). In style they are to be located in Western Asia Minor (probably in southern Phrygia) and indicate that the same early Christian imagery was used there as in Rome in the catacombs and on the sarcophagi.

In northern Phrygia (north-west Turkey) some tomb reliefs which are completely in the earlier tradition of this district have engraved crosses and inscriptions (second half of the third century; pl.30.1); these show that they were made for Christian patrons. They dispense with the figured decoration customary in the workshop, namely standing figures, busts or lions, or the portal of a tomb.

Above all in Rome, but also in Aquileia and Trier, tombstones with an inscription and also figured and decorative adornment were popular. They are difficult to put in any chronological order since there are no external dates, stylistic criteria cannot be applied, and even the form of lettering or the content of the inscriptions do not give us any precise points of reference. However, a number of pieces in Rome should probably be dated as early as the period before

Constantine; these include the tombstone of Eutropos (now in Urbino, diag.42; pl.27.2).

Constantine and later

'Historical reliefs'. The arch of Constantine in Rome, which was given to the city for the victorious emperor by the senate in 312 CE continues the tradition of Roman honorific and triumphal arches and is even now an impressive monument of late antiquity in the 'eternal city'. Unlike the arch of the emperor Galerius, which was erected in 297–305 CE in Thessaloniki, the arch of Constantine is not all of a piece. Predominantly, earlier material has been used, namely reliefs which come from buildings of the emperors Trajan, Hadrian and Antoninus Pius. The low long friezes which are the basis for determining the style of this period and thus also the early Constantinian sarcophagi are above all to be dated to the years 312–315. Characteristic of them are the small figures at the bottom, disproportionate and put close together, the sharp drilled folds, almost drawn, in the garments and the sketched-out hair.

The remains of historical reliefs from the period after the inauguration of the new capital Constantinople have not survived. The columns in the Forum of Constantine which are still standing today bear no decoration. From a later time mention might be made of the remains of a column with reliefs which the emperor Theodosius had erected (386–393); the reliefs on the pedestal of the obelisk which was erected on the Spina (the middle strip) of the hippodrome around 390 (pl.27.3); the column of Arcadius, the son and successor of Theodosius, which was begun in 402 in the forum of Arcadius and has no longer survived, but is known through old drawings; and the pedestal of the column of Marcian (450–452), on the side of which two Nikes are depicted.

Statues. Already in the third century CE the making of copies of famous Greek works had considerably declined. It seems largely to have stopped in the late third or fourth century. The last large-scale sculptures known to us are the two Dioscuri, reining their horses, now on the Quirinal in Rome, which come from the baths founded by Constantine (c.330 CE).

The few later copies include the gallery of herms which was put up in the villa of Welschbillig near Trier (c.375/380). They include copies of earlier works, e.g. heads of philosophers, emperors and ideal statues. The bronze group of Christ healing the woman with an issue of blood in the city of Caesarea Philippi (Paneas) which is described by Eusebius (*History* VII, 18) is probably an earlier group of Apollo and Daphne which has merely been renamed. The report that Constantine the Great had a statue of Christ erected in the imperial palace in Constantinople is very late and is hardly to be trusted. We have no idea what the life-size silver figures (Christ, apostles, angels) which Constantine donated for the 'Fastigium' (perhaps a magnificient screen separating off the sanctuary) of the Salvator Church (S.Giovanni in Laterano) looked like.

The group of small-scale 'table feet' extends down to the fourth century; but no clearly Christian example has been identified, and nothing is known of their original use. Some small decorative statues have been preserved from the fourth century which will have served as decoration for houses. These include e.g. Ganymede with the eagle, an Eros–Psyche group, and an Artemis or Aphrodite statuette. Whether these were bought by members of the old religion or by Christians must remain open.

Portraits. Compared with the second and third century CE, the number of portrait statues and busts decreases sharply, but they continue to be made, at least into the sixth century. They are of emperors and empresses and of private persons; honorific statues on public streets and places were made for them and also tomb statues and busts, as in the early period of the empire. It is much more difficult to date the portraits than in the first to third century CE, since the portraits of empresses and emperors on coins which provide the basis for the chronology are so generalized in the later period that they provide very little basis for putting the statues in order. Nor can very much be done with stylistic criteria. The series to be followed runs from various portraits of Constantine the Great through excellent busts of a couple of the Theodosian period in Thessalonika, the so-called Gratian in Trier, the so-called Arcadius in Istanbul and some impressive heads of the fifth century, to the so-called Theodora (in Milan) and the so-called Justinian (in Venice).

Portrait statues, predominantly of men, often without heads, are known above all from Rome, Constantinople, Ephesus and Aphrodisias. Sometimes the figures are wearing a toga, the dress of the Roman citizen (pl.28.1), but sometimes also the chlamys, the dress of officials (pl.28.2). Sometimes those portrayed have a napkin (*mappa*) clasped in their hand and thus indicate that they had a public function, for example opened games. In various porphyry statues the man is portrayed with a short garment and a breastplate, i.e. as a senior military leader. These may have been statues of emperors. The bronze equestrian statue of the emperor Justinian which was erected in Constantinople in 543/544 and has only survived in a drawing was extraordinarily large (three to four times life-size); possible an earlier statue was reused.

Many examples show that in the fourth century – and perhaps even later – it was customary to reuse old statues and simply indicate their new purpose by changing an inscription or adding a new one. One example is the statue of Scholasticia seated; this evidently rich woman had baths in Ephesus restored in the fourth century CE, and the statue erected there in her honour comes from the second century CE. In the fourth century, merely a new inscription was added to the pedestal; we do not know whether the head, which has not survived, was exchanged, altered or simply left.

Reliefs. A number of reliefs bear Christian representations (e.g. in Istanbul, Athens, Carthage, Berlin and Nicosia); we do not know their original use. Several local Syrian pieces show the saint Simeon Stylites. The relief icons form a special group. New discoveries in Hagios Polyeuktos in Istanbul (at least Christ and the twelve apostles) which was built in 524–527 CE confirm that these were not first made in the Middle Ages, but were already common in the early Christian and early Byzantine period. The original installation is not known. Perhaps they were fixed to the *templon* (the barrier before the sanctuary); the description of the *templon* of Hagia Sophia, which indicates that it was decorated with silver shields on which Christ, Mary, angels, prophets and apostles were depicted, could indicate this.

A few reliefs show pagan or 'neutral' depictions, e.g. Heracles (in Ravenna, pl.30.2) or children at play (now in Berlin). They could come from the private sphere and have served as the decoration of prominent houses or palaces. Probably in the late fourth century the temple of Hadrian in Ephesus was restored and had a frieze with figures attached; it is one of the very rare testimonies to clearly pagan artistic activity at this time. Around 500 CE the emperor commissioned two pedestals for statues (which are lost) of the famous charioteer Porphyrius on the Spina (central axis) of the hippodrome in Constantinople (in Istanbul).

Table tops. A group of marble panels, the borders of which are decorated with flat reliefs with figures, come very close together (later fourth and early fifth century). Most of them may originate in the eastern Mediterranean and may have been distributed from there. They have scenes from the Old and New Testaments and hunts, rare sea creatures and Dionysian subjects, with Greek myths as an exception. We do not know the original use of any example. Perhaps some stood in churches; most may have belonged to decorative tables in private houses.

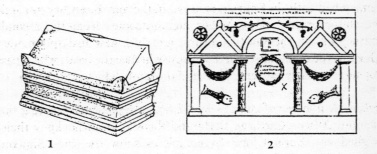

44. Early Christian plastic art: 1. reliquary (fourth/fifth century, length c.0.20/0.30 m); 2. tomb from Asia Minor (near Konya, Turkey, fourth century?, 1.22 x 1.55 m).

Reliquaries. Stone reliquaries form a special group. Most of them have the form of small sarcophagi with a roof lid (diag.44.1). The material is predominantly marble, but in Syria basalt or limestone. Mostly they are simple and only decorated at the edges. In many examples in Syria there are openings in the lid through which oil could be poured into the reliquary; it touched the relics and flowed out again at the front or on the side, where it could be collected by the faitfhful and taken home in ampoulles. Some reliquaries have crosses on the chests and/or lids. Only a few are elaborate: one in

Sivas (north-eastern Turkey) with a lamb on one long side; one in Berat (Albania) with decoration on all four sides; the most splendid one, in Ravenna, has figurative scenes from the New Testament on all four sides (mid-fifth century, pl.27.1).

Inscriptions. These offer rich source material for early Christianity and pose their own problems, so they require specialist treatment by epigraphists. However, two groups can be brought into the sphere of art. One is the group of monumental inscriptions which Pope Damasus (366–384) had attached to the tombs of many martyrs in the catacombs and cemeteries around Rome. They are composed in hexameters in the style of Virgil and written in carefully executed majuscules which in form go back to the first century CE; these are chiselled on marble panels. Great importance was attached to excellent artistic execution.

The second group comprises private epitaphs which, while more or less rapidly executed, have additional decorations. A series of examples is widely distributed in Asia Minor but cannot be dated more precisely. Tomb monuments in the form of low blocks from around Konya (central Turkey, diag.44.2) are unusual. They derive from pagan altar ostothekes (tombstones in the form of a block) in this area; most have a tripartite architectonic division with gables and arches and bear various kinds of decorations: vine-patterns and fishes, and in one case a fish with Jonah.

In the West of the empire, above all in Rome but also in Aquileia (northern Italy), Gaul and Trier, a large number of inscriptions have been preserved which are enriched by decorations or scenes with figures. These engravings are quite flat, and only in exceptions is there deep relief. In Rome they are usually on the rectangular slabs with which tombs (*loculi*) in the catacombs were sealed. In addition there are some upright rectangular pieces which have been used in another way. The representations are very different in character and have some parallels on the sarcophagi and in the paintings of the catacombs, but have been executed much more rapidly. The tombstone of Eutropos, which is now preserved in Urbino but comes from the Catacombs of SS.Marcellino e Pietro in Rome, shows very vividly the making of a sarcophagus and is one of the finest examples (diag.42; pl.27.2).

As the execution of most pieces is very cursory, it is not possible to propose precise dates. Perhaps some, e.g. the Eutropos tombstone (pl.27.2), were already made in the time before Constantine. One example is dated 338, another 408 CE; but we have no points of contact for attaching other pieces to these in a relative sequence, as the craftsmanship is very simple.

The tombstones in Aquileia have different forms. Praying figures are very numerous in the subjects, but we also find e.g. a smith at work and a baptism. In Gaul the repertoire seems to be limited to birds, vine-patterns and different kinds of crosses. Only a few of the very numerous epitaphs in Trier have decorations, almost always birds beside a cross or another motif. The tombstones in the three areas can be put into the fourth and above all the fifth centuries.

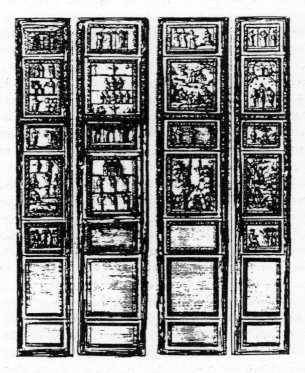

45. Rome, S.Sabina: wooden door panels (c.430); drawing from the year 1756 (height c.5.30 m, width c.3.10 m); cf. pl.31.3.

Wood reliefs. Only a few fragments remain of a further genre of sculpture which once must have been very numerous, namely church doors carved from wood and bearing reliefs. There are small fragments in Milan (end of fourth century) and Cairo (c.500). Despite some losses and many additions, the door panels of S.Sabina in Rome (c.430, pl.29.3) give a good idea. In the original arrangement scenes from the Old Testament and the New Testament were put side by side. In addition there were richly decorated ornaments. The subjects are extremely important, since they give an idea of the distribution of Christian art. For example they include the earliest depiction of the crucifixion of Christ. The doors will at one time have been painted, but we have no idea of their original appearance.

VI

Small-scale Art

Small-scale art comprises various objects made of different materials: liturgical utensils and garments, representative gifts, luxury articles, things for daily use, coins, etc. The main materials are ivory, silver, more rarely gold, frequently bronze, glass, different kinds of stones, clay, wood, material made of wool or silk. The craftsmanship of some objects is very simple; others are artistically highly significant and many pieces are among the masterpieces of their time.

Two points are important in assessing small-scale art: first, as a rule it is very difficult to determine the place of manufacture, as the objects could be transported over long distances. Moreover, in many groups it was also easy for the artist to change his abode. For example, someone who carved ivory needed few tools in addition to the material, so he could travel without great expense from Alexandria or Constantinople to Trier if he saw possibilities of earning money there. To give just one example, the famous ivory pyx in Berlin could have been made by an itinerant or an immigrant artist, but it could also have been imported in a finished state from Alexandria, Constantinople or another place. Secondly, the number of extant pieces in individual materials varies considerably. Silver or gold, for example, were often later melted down and reused. We only have chance examples which have been buried and rediscovered. Glass and earthenware survive in the ground very well for centuries; by contrast, wood and fabric are almost always lost, and are preserved only in favourable climatic conditions, almost exclusively in Egypt. So we only have a tiny proportion of the rich church treasures which we can infer from many mentions in literature. We probably have proportionately more ivory, since it can be reused only to a limited degree; for example, another relief could be cut on the back of an ivory tablet.

In these works of small-scale art, on the one hand we find Christian scenes; some pieces could have been used in church, but as a rule they will have been private property; that also applies, for example, to objects decorated with christograms or the names of apostles. On the other hand, pagan representations are frequent; sometimes they may have been used quite deliberately by members of the pagan opposition as propaganda (e.g. a number of ivories and silver plates, and also the contorniates); but these representations were predominantly pictures and were also bought or commissioned by Christians. Some works of small-scale art are of great importance for early Christian iconography; others give us some knowledge of lost pieces from Graeco–Roman antiquity.

There is hardly any evidence of Christian small-scale art from the period before Constantine. The pictures of a dove, a fish, a ship or anchor, a fisherman and a lyre recommended by Clement of Alexandria as seals around 210 are 'neutral'. Gems with Jonah and a ship (now in London) could come from before the time of Constantine; however, they cannot be dated accurately. A clay lamp with the 'good shepherd', the ark and Jonah seems to come from a workshop which can be dated around 200 CE (in Berlin, diag.49.2).

1. Ivory (and bone)

Ivory is got from the tusks of male Indian and more rarely African elephants. In late antiquity down to the sixth century, the art of carving blocks and cylindrical containers of ivory bearing figures was in its heyday. Among works in ivory are many masterpieces of the early Christian period which were made for members of the top levels of society.

The consular diptychs (pl.29.1; dated after 395) are particularly important. They are usually dated and can be followed from around 395 to 540 CE; they thus provide points of contact for classifying other ivories and further works of small-scale art. These are tablets connected by hinges (diptychon) on the insides of which the new consuls or other high officials announced to colleagues in office and dignitaries their accession to office (the original inscriptions are always lost). The outsides were decorated with various kinds of representations. Those which show the consul enthroned at the opening of the circus races, animal baiting or theatre performances which he gave at his accession are particularly impressive. The consular diptychs and related pieces were made in Constantinople and Rome and perhaps in other places.

Various diptychs with pagan themes (e.g. Asclepius and Hygieia, muse and poet) display exquisite work in 'classical' style which quite deliberately borrows from much older works. They were probably commissioned by members of the pagan opposition and used as gifts to indicate the ongoing importance of the old gods and to hark back to the heyday of the Roman empire. They include the diptychon of the Nichomachi and Symmachi which was perhaps made on the occasion of a marriage (end of the fourth century, now in London and Paris).

There are also diptychs with Christian scenes, but we do not know what they were originally used for. They include the two exquisite tablets in Berlin with Mary enthroned and Christ (pl.29.2; middle of the sixth century). Often the tablets are not all of a piece but are composed of five parts, a large rectangle in the middle and narrow strips at the sides, above and below ('five-part' diptychs). In no case has the original use of these diptychs been preserved. Perhaps some were book bindings, but in others the relief is very high.

Among the pyxes there are several with pagan representations which could have served as jewellery caskets. Most of those with Christian themes will also have been used privately at home. Perhaps they also served to contain consecrated bread. A relatively large number of pyxes have been preserved, as they were frequently used in the Middle Ages as caskets for relics and were included in church treasuries. The 'Berlin pyx' (c.400 CE) is of outstanding quality. One typical example is the pyx found in Trier with three scenes from the Old Testament including the three young men in the fiery furnace (pl.29.3; second half of the fifth century). Two larger rectangular caskets, perhaps reliquaries, are special cases: the 'Lipsanotheca' of Brescia, with an unusually rich programme of pictures from the Old and New Testaments (c.360/370), and the Pola casket, depicting screens in churches which are perhaps to be related to Constantinian foundations in Rome (now in Venice, first half of the fifth century). A relatively large and thick rectangular piece, the 'Trier Ivory', may have been the front of a casket; it shows the transfer of relics – in a casket! – to a newly-built church; perhaps the casket was sent with relics from Constantinople to Trier (Trier, cathedral treasury, fifth century?).

The most splendid work in ivory is the cathedra (throne) which Archbishop Maximian of Ravenna (546–556) commissioned. The wooden frame is clad in numerous ivory panels which in outstanding work show the apostles standing and scenes from the legend of Joseph and the life of Christ.

A very large number of works in ivory have been preserved from the early period. But we must always remember that the painting, which was quite decisive for their original appearance, has now completely disappeared. All the pieces may have been coloured; mediaeval ivories can give some indication.

With most works in ivory – apart from the consular diptychs –the problem of place of manufacture arises. So far there is no viable basis for classification, so sometimes there are very different conjectures for localization.

Instead of ivory, which was very expensive, bone was also used for carvings, but artistically these are much more modest. Evidently the craftsman were far from having the ability of the ivory carvers, and the material was much coarser. Particular note should be taken of caskets with various representations which were used privately at home (known above all from Egypt).

In the Middle Ages, both in the Byzantine empire and the West, ivory had a great heyday; often these works are related to early Christian and early Byzantine ones.

2. Silver

In the early Christian period silver was very often used both for profane and for sacred objects. Sometimes parts of surfaces were gilded. Goblets and cups were imperial gifts on the jubilees of reigns or other special occasions, and these could bear the head of the ruler or full-figure portrayals. The most famous piece is the 'missorium' ('great plate') of Theodosius of 388, which shows the emperor enthroned with his sons (in Madrid). Numerous plates, goblets and dishes, but also flagons, are adorned with figures which are predominantly taken from the world of Graeco–Roman art. Some of these are perhaps gifts; this may be how the 'Kaiseraugst treasure' (in Augst near Basel) came to be collected. Often, too, a large number of the pieces will have been commissioned or acquired for adorning a home, villa or private palace appropriately with precious objects to show the culture of the owner; perhaps the 'Seuso treasure' is a coherent ensemble of such commissioned work. The Esquiline treasure (now in London) from the late fourth century may have been a wedding present.

On some pieces of silver, pagan scenes are depicted quite demonstratively, e.g. on the Parabiago plate (in Milan), the Corbridge Lanx (in London) and pieces of the Mildenhall find (in London). Perhaps these were given as gifts by members of the pagan opposition and were meant to keep the old world of the gods alive.

Silver seems to have been the preferred material for liturgical utensils after the second half of the fourth century, as is shown by the many examples which have been preserved. There are patens (plates), goblets, fans (*ripidi, flabella*), lamps, containers for incense, flagons and reliquiaries (pl.28.3; in Paris, fifth century) of different forms, and perhaps also book covers. Some have figures on them, others only crosses; many are simple. Even churches in small remote towns seem to have had rich stores of silver vessels.

Silver spoons, of which many have survived, were in private use; often they bear christograms or the names of apostles.

Silver objects from the east of the empire often have a control stamp with details of the reigning emperor, by which they are precisely dated. The series can be followed from Anastasius I (491–518) to Constans II (641–668). This also provides certain points of contact for dating other genres of small-scale art.

In the Middle Ages silver increasingly lost significance; it was replaced by gold.

3. Gold

Gold was used almost exclusively in the profane sphere, for jewellery. Armlets, rings, girdles (including wedding girdles), medallions which will have served as pendants, more or less elaborate necklaces and ear-rings have been found. The pieces are often decorated with coloured stones and exceptionally with enamel. Some bear Christian representations. Gold girdle clasps and pins (for fastening garments) which were given by emperors to persons in high office, and for example also to barbarian rulers as special distinctions, comparable to an order, are exceptional cases. Only very rarely are liturgical vessels made of gold. Mention should also be made of some chalices and various small reliquaries.

In the Middle Ages gold became extremely important as a material for precious liturgical vessels and utensils and was widespread, both in the Byzantine empire and in the West. In the early Middle Ages the technique of enamelling was increasingly refined, and in the high Middle Ages splendid work was made in East and West.

4. Bronze

Since it was a cheap material in the early Christian period, bronze was used very often for profane and sacred pieces of small-scale art, predominantly cast, and more rarely wrought. There are dishes, flasks, ladles and so on, objects for everyday use, weights for scales including some with the bust of an imperial figure (pl.30.3 Munich, fifth century), and even decorations. The hanging and standing lamps, which took many forms, are a major group. A large number of wrought fittings for wooden caskets have been preserved from Pannonia (Hungary) and the Rhine area (Mainz, Bonn, Cologne). They were produced with the help of models which made production in series possible: the caskets were used to keep jewellery and other precious objects in. Pieces from the fourth century bear on the one hand a bust in a tondo, and on the other scenes from the New Testament and Old Testament in rectangular fields.

Crosses which stood, were held in the hand or hung as pendants were intended for private and church use. 'Polykandela' of various sizes probably served as lamps only in sacred rooms; they were a kind of circular lampstand in which glass lamps with oil in were put. Cast containers for incense which are among the earliest examples with cycles from the New Testament (sixth/seventh century) depicted on them are an important group; they were probably brought by pilgrims from the Holy Land as souvenirs.

Small figures cast of bronze are rare. They include figures of gods, the emperor Constantine on a horse, Heracles, Peter with a large cross, and Odysseus on a ship and on horseback. Some belonged to carriages or ships. A gilded bust of an emperor could have been the centre of a dish and have come to the Danube as a gift from Constantinople (now in Budapest).

Some objects in which recesses have been made in the bronze and filled with slivers of other material – silver, copper and sometimes niello – must have been very valuable. A small group seems to have been made in Italy (in Rome? during the second half of the fourth century). Where a contorniate found in Trier made by this technique was manufactured must remain open.

5. Other metals

Rarely, we have small-scale objects of other metals. One important group consists of flasks made of a lead-tin alloy (sixth or early seventh

46. Flasks in Monza (northern Italy) which come from Palestine, made of a lead-tin alloy (height c.19 cm): 1. Christ on the cross between the soldiers playing dice; below, the women at the tomb; 2. Ascension of Christ.

century). They were bought by pilgrims in the Holy Land and, filled with consecrated oil, brought back home as souvenirs. Since a number of them are in the treasury of the church of Monza (in northern Italy), they are also known as Monza flasks (diag.46). The representations reflect those on monuments and thus they are among the most important evidence of artistic creativity of the time before the iconographic dispute (726–843), since the large monuments have been destroyed. A brass flagon which shows the adoration of the magi in wrought work could be such a pilgrim souvenir (in Bonn, seventh century?).

6. Glass

It was already known how to make glass in Egypt in the third and second millennia BCE. From the eighth century BCE a large quantity of it appears in Phoenicia, and it was largely traded on from there. Later, glass was made in many areas of the Mediterranean. Production expanded greatly in the first century BCE when the glass blowing pipe was invented, so that glass could be blown in moulds or freely. From then on it became an everyday object rather than a luxury item. There are many simple pieces in late antiquity; but now various techniques of producing particularly valuable glass developed.

Gilded glass. Two types can be distinguished. In the first, which is rare, gold leaves are stuck to the outside of the glass without a protective layer and designs are then engraved on it. This group includes the 'Blue Dish' from Cologne/Braunsfeld and St Ursula's Dish in Cologne (in Cologne or London, first half of the fourth century). In the second, the gold foil is inserted between two layers of glass; the result is 'layered gold glass', which was considerably more durable than the other kind. As a rule gold leaf was let into the bottom of a dish in which a representation was engraved and cut. In earlier examples from the second and third centuries the scenes are painted on the foil in colour; the most splendid example of this is a dish on which a rider called Alexander is portrayed hunting (in Cleveland, middle of the third century). There are various pagan, Jewish and a great many Christian subjects (pl.32.3), which were evidently produced side by side in the same work-shops, above all in Rome, perhaps also in Cologne and Trier. A dish with several gilded glass bosses, bearing scenes from the Old Testament and New Testament, which was found in St Severin, Cologne, is quite unusual (in London, second half of the fourth century).

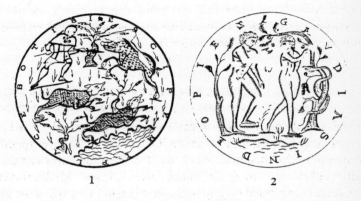

47. Engraved glass from the Wint Hill group produced in a workshop in Cologne (middle of fourth century): 1. with a hunt (diameter 18.5 m); 2. with Adam and Eve, the tree and the serpent (diameter 20 cm); cf. pl.32.2.

Engraved glass. Here, too, there are different groups. In the 'Wint Hill Group', which was made in Cologne, the outlines of the figures are emphasized by parallel strokes. On the one hand there are pagan subjects, hunts (diag.47.1) and mythological scenes; and on the other Christian subjects (diag.47.2; pl.32.2). Thus the workshop worked for various patrons (above all in the second quarter of the fourth century). The 'Rodenkirchen group' clearly differs in the engraving technique (second half of the fourth century). Here, too, there are pagan subjects, many of them Dionysian, and Christian subjects. The famous Cologne circus dish belongs to this group (now in Cologne). The place of manufacture is unknown; it could be Cologne or a centre further south. The 'Igelkopf group' may have been made in Cologne. Christian scenes – the details of which are hard to interpret – are particularly frequent (second half of the fourth century).

Diatrete glass ('cage cups'). Most valuable of all are 'diatretes', in which usually filigree (diag.51.1) and in very rare cases figures have been engraved in the originally thick wall of the glass. There may have been workshops for the filigree examples in Cologne and probable also in Trier. Extant pieces come from the fourth century. Fragments were found in the imperial palace in Trier and the imperial villa in Konz.

Mould-blown glass. This technique made possible the manufacture of series and was known from the late first century CE. In late antiquity, among other objects, small flasks were made which pilgrims could bring back, filled with oil, as souvenirs of places in the Holy Land.

The fragment of a glass statuette of a woman (now in New York) and the bust of a prince which will have been the middle of a dish (now in Cologne), both from the fourth century CE, are special cases.

7. Cut stones

Most of the small-scale stone pieces can be divided into three groups. 1. Gems (intaglio); with these the decor is set into the surface; very varied kinds of stone have been used. 2. Cameos; these have a high relief and as a rule are worked out of stones with several coloured layers. 3. Statues in the round and vessels of precious and decorated stones.

Gems. A distinction has to be made between 'seal gems' (used for seals), in which the designs and in some cases inscriptions are the wrong way round, and 'magical gems' . The gems for seals stand in a very old tradition and are numerous in Greek and Roman time. Production of them declined sharply during the third century CE, and there are just a few examples in the fourth century. The earliest seals, perhaps used by Christians, cannot be recognized since – as e.g. Clement of Alexandria advised around 210 CE – they have 'neutral' designs: dove, fish, ship, heron, anchor or fisherman. They were obviously for sale, and not specially made for Christians. Some of these gems have Christian inscriptions or bear a christogram; there is much to indicate that such items were later partly 'Christianized' or are even modern forgeries. The very few gems known with subjects from the New Testament and the Old Testament show a reduced version of the usual iconography; the execution is modest.

Some well-wrought gems with portraits of the emperor, and perhaps the seal of the ruler of the time (e.g. gems in Berlin and London which probably depict Constantine the Great), are exceptions. Some gems of a rather larger size and with inscriptions the right way round could have served as amulet pendants: examples are the healing of the woman with an issue of blood (in New York) and the bust of Christ on a cross, flanked by Peter and Paul (in Vienna), both of which probably come from the east of the empire (sixth century BCE).

The 'magical gems' form a large group above all in the second and third century CE. They were meant to protect the owners from disaster, bring them luck, diminish birth pains, secure the favour of the beloved, and so on. It is difficult to date these pieces precisely, since the craftsmanship is usually very simple, but some could have been made in the fourth century. They seem predominantly to come from Egypt and often depict Egyptian deities, usually as strange hybrid beings.

Cameos. These are often made of several layers of sardonyx and were worked so that the darker layer forms the background and lighter layers form the figures standing out in high relief. Smaller pieces may have served as rings or pendants. The larger ones were works of court art and gifts either given to the emperor or made for the emperor to give to persons in high office. A series of excellent pieces has been preserved from the period of the Roman empire. The cameos of late antiquity include the 'Ada Cameo' (in Trier), which perhaps depicts Constantine and his family and was made before 326; the once very large sardonyx with a battle scene, probably from the time of Constantine (now in Belgrade); a fragment with busts of women arranged around a head in the centre, probably of the same period (in Cologne); possibly the 'Hague Cameo', which could also have been made in the time of Constantine, but which is strongly rooted in the earlier tradition (in The Hague); and an exquisite piece which was perhaps made on the occasion of the wedding of Honorius at the end of the fourth century (in Paris).

After a long gap cameos evidently flourished again to some degree in the early Byzantine period. Some examples have been preserved which served as pendants (*enkolpia*) and show the annunciation to Mary, the adoration of the cross, etc. Cameos were made in the Middle Ages both in Constantinople and in the West.

Statues in the round, vessels. Statues in the round made from precious stones must be regarded as exceptionally valuable pieces. Mention should be made of busts of the emperors (including one of Constantine the Great) made of agate (now in Paris); a statuette of Heracles (now in Baltimore); a miniature temple (now in New York); a dish decorated with fish (now in Venice); or two lion's heads (probably from Trier, now in Paris), all of which are made of rock crystal (probably fourth century CE).

Among the very few vessels from late antiquity made of precious stones, an agate dish (from Trier, in Vienna) and the 'Rubens Vase', decorated with rich vine patterns and heads of Pan, which was for a while in the possession of P.P.Rubens (now in Baltimore), stand out; they are probably both from the fourth century CE.

8. Textiles

A tremendous quantity of textiles must have been produced all over the Roman empire in the early Christian period. They have survived almost exclusively in Egypt, where they were put into tombs and did not decay because of the dry climate. Garments, curtains and wall-hangings with decorative and figured decoration are particularly important for the sphere of art.

The materials used were linen and wool, and also valuable silk which in late antiquity and the early Christian period had to be imported from Persia; only in 552 did it prove possible to get silkworms in the Byzantine empire and begin production there. The materials are decorated with various techniques. Sometimes, above all in the case of silk, figures and background details are woven in; here we often find sequences of small scenes which relate to one another. Linen was in part coloured by 'reserve technique', a technique already described by Pliny the Great (who died in 79 CE). Some material of this kind has rich cycles from the New and Old Testaments; sometimes it was originally in a large format and served as wall hangings. Some large-format material with figures woven into it has also been preserved. In garments, stripes (*clavi*), rectangles or medallions with figured and/or ornamental decoration are woven into the fabric by various techniques, or sewn on to it. Sometimes the use of a rod in weaving produces tufts around 2 cm long (nap). In very rare cases the designs are painted. Mummy cloths from Egypt from the time of the empire contain forerunners of this.

There will also have been comparable textiles in other areas of the Roman empire. This is attested e.g. by wall paintings in Rome and mosaics in Ravenna, which clearly show that the figures have richly decorated garments. A sermon by Bishop Asterius of Amaseia, a provincial city in northern Asia Minor, also belongs in this context: it is opposed to luxury in dress and mentions many of the scenes depicted (late fourth century).

Sack-like garments with long sleeves were widespread (*tunica*, diag.48). Braid and medallions or rectangles were woven into more elaborate garments. Numerous scenes from Greek mythology and Christian subjects are depicted in strong colours.

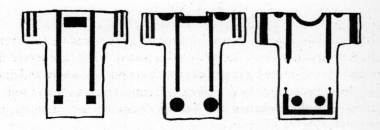

48. Tunics (garments) of late antiquity with different forms of embroidery.

Larger-format textiles are particularly valuable. Some could have served as curtains, others may have been wall hangings in rich private houses and in churches or other sacred buildings. Several show scenes from the Graeco–Roman world, above all from the Dionysius cycle, others individual scenes or even cycles from the Old and New Testaments.

As exceptions, mention should be made of fabrics which give the effect of being monumental icons and perhaps also served as such. Because of its size, strong colours and good preservation, the large example in Cleveland woven from wool (sixth century) is particularly impressive. The enthroned Mother of God, flanked by two angels with the ascension of Christ above her, is depicted in a rich frame. A similar fabric could have hung in a church in Palestine and have incurred the wrath of the iconoclastic bishop Epiphanius of Salamis on Cyprus, who tore it down (c.393 CE).

It is very difficult to date the textiles. On the one hand they come from one province of the Roman empire, Egypt, and on the other they are usually products with simple craftsmanship which can only to a very limited degree be connected with other works of small-scale art. So the conjectures to be found in the literature must always be taken only as approximate dates.

The textiles are very important, first because they tell us something about the everyday life of the early Christians; second, because they attest the ongoing existence of pagan designs well down into late antiquity; and third, because in part they copy monumental cycles, probably of wall paintings, with scenes from the Old Testament and New Testament.

9. Clay

As already in former times, so too in late antiquity all over the Roman empire utensils were made from clay, above all plates, cups, dishes, pots, jugs and storage vessels of various sizes. As a rule they were simple and only sometimes decorated with fluting or lips. However, attention should be drawn to some groups. Vessels were made, probably in Trier, with a 'Barbotine' technique. Here plant decorations, large inscriptions and so on were painted on the black varnished ground with thick white slicks which were sometimes coloured yellow; sometimes there are also pressed relief panels which have been coloured. Finds indicate that these unusual pieces were worked between the middle of the third and the middle of the fourth centuries.

Lamps often have a small field with figured relief on the upper side. One example with a Christian subject may date from before the time of Constantine (in Berlin, diag.49.2). Numerous of them have survived from the later fourth and also the fifth century. There are

49. Lamps from the early Christian period: 1. with Christogram and ornaments (fourth/fifth centuries); 2. with Noah's ark, Jonah and the 'Good Shepherd' (third century; length 15.2 cm).

crosses (diag.49.1) and sometimes also scenes with figures.

In some of the pilgrimage centres, ampoules (small flat flasks with two handles) were made of clay for pilgrims to take home consecrated water or oil in. The representations on both sides of the body recall the saints visited, e.g. St Simeon (Syria) and St Menas (Egypt, diag.502), a warrior hero unknown to us, or St Thecla (southern Asia Minor, diag.50.1).

Products from workshops in western North Africa, present-day Tunisia, striking because of their red colour and manufactured in series (Terra Sigillata Chiara C), are widespread in the Mediterranean. Rectangular plates and above all low dishes (predominantly from the second half of the fourth century) have been preserved. They are decorated with flat reliefs; they were pressed in moulds and then impressed on the originally flat objects in different ways so that the individual pieces are very different. The variety of themes is amazing. There are many pagan pictures, e.g. of Hercules, the Egyptian gods and Mithras, and numerous scenes from both the

50. Clay ampoulles (height 8–12 cm): 1. from a sanctuary of Thecla; 2. from the St Menas sanctuary in northern Egypt (fourth/fifth centuries).

New Testament and the Old Testament (pl.32.1); these items were bought by Christians and perhaps also Jews. The same workshops also worked for adherents of different religions. Clay copies were made as imitations of precious silver tablets; in the centre these depict mythological scenes, e.g. Bellerophon or Priam before Achilles; there are also Christian scenes, and even ivory consular diptychs were copied in clay. The conquest of North Africa by the Vandals after 420 CE evidently put an end to the production of this genre.

10. Wood

Wood was certainly used very frequently in the early Christian period, for simpler everyday objects, but also for furniture, caskets and the decoration of houses and churches. Because of the climatic conditions, pieces have been preserved almost exclusively in Egypt; these could be regarded as examples also for other areas of the Roman empire.

Items widespread in the private sphere are: combs, which have sometimes been put in with the dead brand new; flasks for perfume or mascara; mirror holders, weaving combs, stamps, small figures and dolls; and caskets. These objects can have carvings and be painted. Sometimes the middle of the comb is broken.

Numerous fragments show that furniture was also made of wood, decorated with carving and probably also painted; however, the forms cannot be reconstructed. A series of fragments belonged to painted boxes. In their case it must remain open whether they were in private houses or churches. That also applies to parts which were perhaps door beams or could have belonged to doors or screens.

A casket in the Vatican (sixth century?) contains stones from places in the Holy Land and was thus a pilgrim souvenir; it is of quite special significance, since the inside of the lid has five painted scenes from the life of Christ which are among the earliest of their kind. Other chests could also have been pilgrim souvenirs, e.g. one in Berlin the outside of which is painted (sixth century).

11. Coins and contorniates

The coins are also important sources for the history of late antiquity. But they pose considerable problems, so that study of them has developed into a specialist area, numismatics. This is because an impossibly large number of them have been preserved; they were minted in numerous places in the empire, not only in Rome and Constantinople but e.g. also in London, Trier, Arles, Nicomedia (Izmit, north–western Turkey), Antioch (Antakya, south–east Turkey) or Carthage; finally the designs on them are very varied and there are many changes. Only a few comments can be made here.

Coins. These are generally made of bronze, and those of higher value of silver or gold. Like earlier coins, those of late antiquity as a rule have the image of the emperor or empress on one side, in profile, looking right; rarely the heads are looking left, and in exceptional cases in three-quarter profile or frontal; these examples were almost all coined from precious metal for a particular occasion and thus were not everyday currency. Medals made of silver or gold were used for jubilees of reigns, victories and other special events; usually they have particularly fine designs and were given as presents.

The portraits are not realistic, but are meant to glorify the emperors and show their divine qualities and their virtues. Those portrayed on them could not be identified without the inscriptions. They wear a laurel wreath or a diadem, sometimes also helmet and breastplate, and from time to time have other insignia. The depictions from earlier coins have been retained on the reverse. These include embodiments of various virtues, gods, including many city gods, the emperor full-figure, standing, enthroned or on horseback. Christian motives appear on the reverse in isolated instances already under Constantine, and then more frequently from the middle of the fourth century CE.

Coins are also important testimony to early Christian art. As they have been preserved in uninterrupted sequence, variations in style can be read off them. Thus, for example, they can help us to recognize the dates of special features of the style of sculptures and changes in style. If we immerse ourselves in study of the small pieces we can see that some coins can almost be regarded as works of art, both their reverses with very different representations and the portraits on the obverse.

Two groups of coins are particularly interesting for early Christian art and should therefore be emphasized. One consists of local bronze mintings of the city of Apameia in Phrygia (western Asia

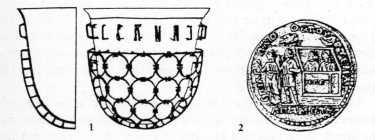

51. Small-scale art from late antiquity: 1. cross-section and sketch of a diatrete glass (middle of the fourth century, height 12 cm); 2. coin from Apameia in Phrygia (western Turkey) with Noah and the ark (c.200, diameter 3.3 cm).

Minor/Turkey) from the time of the emperor Septimius Severus (193–211 CE) to the time of Trebonias Gallus (251–253), in other words a span of around 60 years (diag.51.2). On the obverse they show the likeness of the particular emperor; on the reverse there are depictions of Noah (with inscription) and his wife (a woman) in the ark and a standing pair praying. Reference has been made to a Jewish tradition which locates Mount Ararat near Apameia. Furthermore the city of Apameia bears the name *kibotos*, 'chest', and *kibotos* is also the designation for the ark. Even if Jewish traditions are illustrated here, it is important for Christian graphic art that for the first time we have evidence of the depiction of Noah's ark in a way which later becomes canonical, so the image must have been invented before 200 CE.

In the other group, namely silver medallions which were minted in Ticinum (Pavia) in 313 or 315 CE, the victorious Constantine is depicted on the obverse (pl.32.4). On his helmet he bears the christogram (Chi-Rho sign) which he made as a standard for his army before the battle at the Milvian Bridge in 312 CE. So this medallion, which was issued on the occasion of the victory celebrations, confirms the reports of Lactantius and Eusebius. The medallions are the earliest examples of the use of the Chi-Rho sign. Constantine's entry into Rome was celebrated with a golden medallion, but this is still fully in the pagan tradition (diag.52). On the front it shows an image of the emperor with the sun god Sol, and on the reverse the emperor on horseback: he is led by Victoria, the goddess of victory, and followed by Virtus, the embodiment of bravery. The inscriptions INVICTVS CONSTANTINVS ('invincible Constantine') on the front and FELIX ADVENTVS ('happy arrival') on the back refer to the event. Christian and pagan elements are juxtaposed in many ways in Constantine the Great himself – and not just on the medallions: he first had himself baptized on his deathbed.

Contorniates. These are medallions of copper or more rarely bronze, without monetary value, usually minted, sometimes moulded, large numbers of which were given out by the pagan aristocracy of the city of Rome for propaganda purposes at New Year and probably also for other festivals. They differ from the coins by their thick edge and a deeper line. They begin about 330 CE, are particularly numerous in the second half of the fourth century, and extend to the beginning of the fifth century. The depictions, e.g. pictures of gods and heroes, portraits of emperors and philosophers, pictures from Roman mythology and history, deliberately go back to early models. Along with various ivories and works in silver, the contorniates are a last attempt to promote the old gods, the pre-eminence of Rome and traditional values.

52. Medallion of Constantine the Great, probably minted in 312/313 CE to mark the emperor's entry into Rome after the victory over Maxentius at the Milvian Bridge (diameter 4 cm: Paris, Bibliothèque Nationale).

VII

Museums and Collections with Early Christian Art

Only in the middle of the nineteenth century did people begin to collect objects from the early Christian period. The beginning is marked by the educational collection which F.Piper developed as a 'Christian Museum' at the University of Berlin from 1849. In 1854, within the framework of the papal museums, P.G.Marchi founded a museum in the Lateran Palace which specialized in material from early Christianity. In 1884 V.Schultze established an 'Ecclesiastical-Archaeological Collection' at the University of Greifswald. Finally, in 1904 the 'Early-Christian Byzantine Collection' became an independent division of the Royal Museums in Berlin.

Today there are numerous museums in many countries which have collections from late antiquity, early Christianity and the Byzantine period. The most important are mentioned below, along with a list of the relevant catalogues or guides.

Germany

Berlin, Museum for Late Antiquity and Byzantine Art (formerly the Early Christian-Byzantine Collection): sarcophagi, architectural sculpture, small-scale art, Coptic art; A.Effenberger and H.-G.Severin, *Das Museum für spätantike und byzantinische Kunst*, 1992.
Bonn, Rheinisches Landesmuseum: small-scale art, inscriptions; see below, Exhibition 1991.
Frankfurt, Liebieghaus – Museum alter Plastik: small-scale art and architectural sculpture from Egypt; G. and H.-G.Severin, *Marmor vom heiligen Menas*, 1987.
Cologne, Museum of Roman Germany: glass, ceramics from North Africa, other small-scale art; P.La Baume and J.W.Salomonson, *Römische Klein-kunst der Sammlung Karl Löffler* (n.d), see below, Exhibition 1988.

Mainz, Central Museum of Roman Germany: original pieces of small-scale art and admirable copies; K.Böhner et al., *Das frühe Mittelalter*, ²1980; K.Weidemann, *Spätantike Bilder des Heidentums und Christentums*, 1990; *Von Constantin zu Karl dem Grossen. Denkmäler des Heidentums und Christentums aus der Spätantike*, 1990.

Munich, Prähistorische Staatsammlung: small-scale art, including ceramics from North Africa; see below, Exhibition 1989.

Trier: Episcopal Cathedral and Diocesan Museum: discoveries from excavations in the cathedral including the ceiling paintings; inscriptions, see below, Exhibitions 1964 and 1984; H.Merten, *Die frühchristlichen Inschriften*, 1990.

Trier, Rheinisches Landesmuseum: sarcophagi, glass, ceramics and other small-scale art; see below, Exhibitions 1964 and 1984.

Great Britain

Scattered pieces are discussed in the catalogue of the London exhibition 1994/95; the following museums should be noted:

London, British Museum: large and varied collection; the earlier pieces are in a catalogue, but not the numerous new acquisitions; O.N.Dalton, *Catalogue of Early Christian Antiquities and Objects from the Christian East*, British Museum, 1901; see below, Exhibitions 1977.

Oxford, Ashmolean Museum: M.Mundell Mango, *Catalogue of Late Antique and Byzantine Antiquities in the Ashmolean Museum*, Oxford (in preparation).

France

Numerous of the scattered pieces are included in the catalogue of the Paris Exhibition 1992/93; the following museums are important:

Arles, Musée d'Art Chrétienne: significant collection of early Christian sarcophagi; F.Benoit, *Sarcophages paléochrétiens d'Arles et de Marseille*, 1954; Brenk, 1977, pl.358b; Gaul, 1980, 213ff., no.347; 222, no.364.

Paris, Musée du Louvre: sarcophagi, and small-scale early Christian and Coptic art; E.Coche de la Ferté, *L'Antiquité chrétienne au Musée du Louvre*, 1958; F.Baratte and C.Metzger, *Catalogue des sarcophages en pierre d'époques romaine et paléochrétienne*, 1985; D.Bézaneth, *L'art du métal au debut de l'ère chrétienne*, 1992; see below, Exhibition 1992/93.

Switzerland

Augst, Roman museum: treasury of silver from Augusta Raurica dating from late antiquity; H.A.Cahn et al., *Der spätrömische Silberschatz von Kaiseraugst*, 1984.

Austria

Vienna, Kunsthistorisches Museum: small-scale art from late antiquity and early Christianity; R.Noll, *Kunsthistorisches Museum Wien. Vom Altertum zum Mittelalter*, ²1974.

Italy

Some archaeological museums and church treasuries (e.g. Monza, Bobbio) have various early Christian works, and several larger collections:

Aquileia, Museo Cristiano di Monastero: mosaics, inscriptions, reliefs, small-scale art.

Rome, Museo Nazionale Romano and Museo del Palazzo dei Conservatori: early Christian sarcophagi, covered in Rep.I.

Vatican, Museo Pio Cristiano: very large collection of sarcophagi and inscriptions; J.Ficker, *Die altchristlichen Bildwerke im christlichen Museum des Laterans*, 1890; O.Marucchi, *I monumenti del museo Cristiano Pio Lateranense*, 1920; sarcophagi covered in Rep.I.

Vatican, Biblioteca Apostolica: small-scale art; L.von Matt, *Die Kunstsammlungen der Biblioteca Apostolica Vaticana*, 1969.

Croatia

Porec, Basilica Eufrasiana: architectural sculpture; E.Russo, *Sculture del complesso eufrasiano di Parenzo*, 1991.

Split, Archaeological Museum: architectural sculpture, sarcophagi, small-scale art; *Salona Christiana*, 1994; N.Cambi, *The Good Shepherd Sarcophagus and its Group*, 1994; N.Duval and E.Marin, *Salona I. Catalogue de la sculpture paléochrétienne de Salone*, 1994.

Zagreb, Archaeological Museum: small-scale art; *From the Invincible Sun to the Sun of Justice. Early Christianity in Continential Croatia*, 1994; there are also pieces in other museums.

Serbia

Architectural sculpture and small-scale pieces from various museums are in the catalogue of a special exhibition in Belgrade: D.Srejovic (ed.), *Roman Imperial Towns and Palaces in Serbia*, 1993.

Albania

Architectural decoration from various excavations (e.g. Amantia, Byllis, Balsh, Dyrrachium) and small-scale pieces are mainly preserved in four museums: Durres, Archaeological Museum; Korça, Museum of Mediaeval Albania; Tirana, Archaeological Museum and Museum of National History; some pieces are covered in *Albania. Schätze aus dem Land der Skipetaren*, 1988 (further literature ibid., 174–5), also G.Koch, *Kunst und Kultur im Land der Skipetaren*, 1989 (bibliography ibid., 322–4).

Greece

Early Christian pieces are also on display in many museums near where they were found (e.g. Corinth, Rhodes, Thebes); much is in store. There are larger collections in:
Athens, Byzantine Museum: sculpture, various kinds of small-scale art; there is no catalogue, but many pieces have been published in scattered places.
Thessaloniki, exhibition (temporary) in the 'White Tower' (a very large Byzantine Museum is being built): rich collections of sculpture, small-scale art, paintings from tombs; *Thessalonike. Historia kai Techne*, 1986
Thessaloniki: archaeological collection in the crypt of Hagios Demetrios: architectural decoration from the church; G.A.and A.G.Sotiriou, *He basilike tou Hagiou Demetriou Thessalonikes*, 1952.

Russia

St Petersburg, Hermitage: sculpture, extensive collection of small-scale art, including numerous pieces of silver; A.Bank, *Byzantine Art in the Collections of Soviet Museums* (1977, 1985); see also below, Exhibition, Berlin 1977/78.

Ukraine

Cherson, Museum: see Russia, St Petersburg (A.Bank).

Turkey

Objects from the early Christian period have been preserved in almost all the provincial museums (e.g. Adana, Bursa, Iznik, Kayseri, Konya, Silifke); often these are unusual pieces. Some museums have larger collections:

Antakya: mosaics from the excavations in ancient Antioch and its villa suburb of Daphne (other mosaics from the excavations are in Paris and the USA); D.Levi, *Antioch Mosaic Pavements*, 1957.

Antalya: parts of the silver treasury of Kumluca; mosaics, architectural sculpture (some included in *Anatolian Civilizations*, see Istanbul).

Istanbul, Archaeological Museum (at present little on display): numerous sarcophagi and architectural sculptures, several pieces of small-scale art; *The Anatolian Civilizations II. Greek, Roman, Byzantine*, 1983; N.Firatli, *La sculpture byzantine figurée au Musée Archéologique d'Istanbul*, 1990.

Selçuk: finds from Ephesus; at present only a few pieces from late antiquity are on display (most are stored).

Syria

In the national museums of Aleppo and Damascus and some local museums there are statues and pieces from buildings, reliquaries, mosaics and small-scale art; in Damascus also the paintings from the Dura Europos synagogue; some pieces are discussed in *Land des Baal. Syrien – Forum der Völker und Kulturen*, 1982, 227ff.; Syrien 1993, 391ff.; *Syrie. Mémoire et civilisation*, Paris 1993.

Jordan

There are numerous mosaics, pieces of small-scale art and architectural sculpture in various museums; surveys can be found in *Byzantinische Mosaiken aus Jordanien*, Schallaburg 1986; Münster and Munich 1987; Berlin 1987/88; *Der Königsweg. 9000 Jahre Kunst und Kultur in Jordanien und Palästina*, Cologne 1987/88, 307ff.

USA

There are individual pieces in many museums (e.g. Corning, Kansas City, Malibu, New Haven, St Louis, Toledo); some have extensive permanent collections. Some of the objects are included in the catalogue of the New York exhibition of 1977/78.

Baltimore, Walters Art Gallery.

Boston, Museum of Fine Arts, see also below, Exhibition 1976/77.

Cleveland, Museum of Fine Art.

Houston, The Menil Collection.

New York, Metropolitan Museum.

Princeton, Art Museum: *Byzantium at Princeton. Byzantine Art and Archaeology at Princeton University*, 1986.

Richmond, Museum of Fine Art: *Art of Late Rome and Byzantium in the Virginia Museum of Fine Arts, Richmond*, by A.Gonosová and C.Kondoleon, 1994.

Washington, Dumbarton Oaks Collection: *Handbook of the Byzantine Collection, Dumbarton Oaks*, 1967; *Catalogue of the Byzantine and Early Medieval Anqtiuities in the Dumbarton Oaks Collection, I. Metalwork, Ceramics, Glass, Glyptics, Paintings*, by M Ross, 1962; *II. Jewelry, Enamels, and Art of the Migration Period*, by M.Ross, 1965; *III. Ivories and Steatites*, by K.Weitzmann, 1972.

Canada

Toronto, University, The Malcove Collection: various small pieces: S.D.Campbell, *The Malcove Collection*, 1985.

Special exhibitions in various countries

There has been a series of exhibitions wholly or partly of art from late antiquity and early Christianity; the catalogues contain important material:

Berlin 1939	*Kunst der Spätantike im Mittelmeerraum. Berlin, Kaiser-Friedrich-Museum*, 1939
Baltimore 1947	*Early Christian and Byzantine Art. The Walters Art Gallery*, 1947
Essen 1962	*Frühchristliche Kunst aus Rom. Villa Hügel, Essen*, 1962
Essen 1963	*Koptische Kunst. Christentum am Nil. Villa Hügel, Essen*, 1962
Trier 1964	*Frühchristliche Zeugnisse im Einzugsgebiet von Rhein und Mosel*, ed. T.K.Kempf and W.Reusch, 1964
Boston 1976/77	*Museum of Fine Arts, Boston. Romans & Barbarians*, 1976

London 1977   *Wealth of the Roman World, Gold and Silver AD 300–700*, ed. J.P.C.Kent and K.S.Painter, 1977

Berlin 1977/78   *Frühbyzantinische Silbergefässe aus der Ermitage*, ed. A.Effenberger et al., 1978

New York 1977/78   *Age of Spirituality. Late Antique and Early Christian Art, Third to Seventh Century*, ed. K.Weitzmann, 1979

Mainz 1980   *Gallien in der Spätantike. Von Kaiser Constantin zu Frankenkönig Childerich*, 1980

Frankfurt 1983/84   *Spätantike und frühes Christentum. Liebieghaus, Museum alter Plastik Frankfurt*, 1983/84

Baltimore 1986   *Silver from Byzantium. The Kaper Koraon and Related Treasures*, by M.Mundell Mango, 1986

Cologne 1988   *Römisch–Germanisches Museum Köln. Glas der Caesaren*, by D.B.Harden et al., 1988

Urbana 1989   *Art and Holy Power in the Early Christian House*, by E.Dauterman Maguire et al., 1989

Munich 1989   *Spätantike zwischen Heidentum und Christentum. Prähistorische Staatssammlung München*, by J.Garbsch and B.Overbeck, 1989

Milan 1990   *Milano capitale dell'impero romano (286–402 d.c)*, 1990

Bonn 1991   *Spätantike und frühes Mittelalter. Ausgewählte Denkmäler im Rheinischen Landesmuseum Bonn*, ed. J.Engemann and C.B.Rüger, 1991

Paris 1992/93   *Byzance. L'art byzantin dans les collections publiques françaises, Musée du Louvre*, 1992/3

Linz, etc. 1993–95   *Syrien. Von der Aposteln zu den Kalifen*, introduction by E.M.Ruprechtsberger, 1993

Split 1994   *Salona Christiana*, ed. E.Marin, 1994

London 1994/95   *Byzantium. Treasures of Byzantine Art and Culture from British Collections*, ed. D.Buckton, 1994

VIII

Bibliographies on Individual Chapters

I. General

3. *Historical dates*: A.Demandt, *Die Spätantike. Römische Geschichte von Diocletian bis Justinian*, 1989; M.Führmann, *Rom in der Spätantike*, 1994.

4. *History of research*: W.Wischmeyer, *Zeitschrift für Kirchengeschichte* 89, 1978, 136–49; Deichmann 1983, 14–45; Effenberger 1986, 11–14, 335; *Spiegel einer Wissenschaft. Zur Geschichte der Christlichen Archäologie vom 16. bis 19.Jahrhundert, dargestellt an Autoren und Büchern*, Bonn 1991; also H.R.Seeliger, *RQ* 87, 1992, 110–15.

II. Architecture

1. *Sacred architecture*: C.Mango, *Byzantinische Architektur*, 1974 = 1986; G.Stanzl, *Längsbau und Zentralbau als Grundthemen der frühchristlichen Architektur*, 1979; Deichmann 1983, 66–88, 236–88; Krautheimer 1986; W.E.Kleinbauer, *Early Christian and Byzantine Architecture. An Annotated Bibliography and Historiography*, 1992; K.Painter (ed.), '*Churches Built in Ancient Times*', *Recent Studies in Early Christian Archaeology*, 1994; N.Gkioles, *Palaiochristianike techne*, Naodomia 1994.

(a) *The phases. (i) Before Constantine*: J.P.Kirsch, *Die römischen Titelkirchen im Altertum*, 1918; H.Kähler, *Die frühe Kirche*, 1972, cf. 12–18 (Herculaneum, etc.); 26–33 (Dura Europos); 38f. (Salona); 40–53 (Aquileia); Deichmann 1983, 66–88; Effenberger 1986, 85–9; Krautheimer 1986, 23–7; C.H.Kraeling, *The Christian Building. The Excavations at Dura Europos, Final Report* VIII 2, 1967; *RBK* I, 1220–30 (Dura Europos); 1230–40 (on the synagogue); TIB 5, 441–3 (Meriamlik); E.Pelekanidou and A.Mentzos, in *Mneme D.Lazaride*, 1990, 597–607 (Philippi); *Ancient Churches Revealed*, 1993, 71–62 (V.Corbo, Capernaum); Lactantius, *De mortibus persecutorum* XIII (Nicomedia); *Monumenta Antiqua Asiae Minoris* I, 1928, 89–91, no. 170 (inscription of Bishop Eugenius of Laodicea); Eusebius, *Church History* VIII 1 (great buildings before the persecution of Diocletian in 303 CE). (ii) *The time of Constantine*: H.Brandenburg, *Roms frühchristliche Basiliken des 4.Jhs.*, 1979; Deichmann 1983, 238–50; Krautheimer 1986, 39–67; Krautheimer 1988, 40–90; Effenberger 1986, 93–137; *RBK* I, 189/90 (Octagon in Antioch), 610–11 (Bethlehem); III, 588–600 (Jerusalem); *Trier 1984*, 161–3, no.61; A.Arbeiter, *Alt-St.Peter in Geschichte und Wissenschaft*, 1988; J.Rasch, *Das Mausoleum bei Tor dei Schiavi in Rom*, 1993; *Ancient Churches Revealed*, 1993, 23–7, 101–17; D.J.Stanley, *DOP* 48, 1994, 257–61 (S.Costanza, not yet taken account of here in the text). (iii) *After Constantine:* Deichmann 1983, 250–88; Effenberger 1986, 193–330; Krautheimer 1986, 68–199; Krautheimer 1988, 91–133; cf. also I e below.

(b) *General literature on the forms of churches and baptisteries*. (i) *Aisleless buildings, T form*: *RBK* III, 992–1021 (Cappadocia); G.Wiessner, *Christliche Kultbauten im Tur Abdin* II, 1982, 1983; IV, 1993. (ii) *Basilicas*: A.K.Orlandos, *He xylostegos palaiochristianike basilike tes mesogeiakes lekanes*, 1952–1957 (basic); *RBK* I, 514–58; IV, 857–9 (Hagios Titos, Gortyn); V, 529–73 (cupola basilicas); Krautheimer 1988, 40–78; J.Christern, *SBK* I, 163–204 (derivation); *Milano 1992*, 203–17 (ambulatory basilicas). (iii) *Centralized buildings*: Krautheimer 1986 (see index under individual buildings); Krautheimer 1988, 81–90 (Church of the Apostles, Constantinople); *RBK* I, 189/90 (Octagon in Antioch); IV, 865–8 (Kissamos, Crete); Stanzl (see 1 above); *AS*, 668f., no. 595 (Toulouse); J.Deckers, *JbAChr* 83, 1988, 25–43 (Cologne, St Gereon); *Syrien 1993*, 91–4 (southern Syria, including the newly excavated round church in Bosra). *Tri-and tetraconches with ambulatory*: W.E.Kleinbauer, *DOP* 27, 1973, 91–114; 41, 1987, 277–93; P.Grossmann, in *Das römisch-byzantinische Ägypten*, 1989, 167–73; I.Travlos, in *Philia Epe eis G.E.Mylonas* I, 1986, 343–7 (Athens); D.Piguet-Panayotova, *JbAChr* 33, 1990, 197–208; A.Karivieri, in *Post-Herulian Athens*, ed. P.Castrén, 1994, 89–113 (Athens). *Square buildings:* G.Wiessner, *Christliche Kultbauten im Tur Abdin* I, 1981; III, 1993. *Baptisteries:* *RBK* I, 460–96; I.E.Bolanake, *Ta palaiochristianika baptesteria tes Hellados*, 1976; *CIAC*, 559–650; M.Falla Castelfranchi, *Baptisteria. Intorno ai più noti battisteri*, 1980.

(c) *The conversion of ancient buildings*: *RBK* II, 1212–15 (Hierapolis); H.Kähler, *Die frühe Kirche*, 1972; G.Amer et al., *Syria* 59, 1982, 253–318 (Qanawat); J.Vaes, *Ancient Society* 15–17, 1984–86, 305–443 (extensive collection); *Trier 1984*, 139ff., no.52 (basilica).

(d) *The parts of the basilica – the furnishing of churches*: Orlandos (see above, b), 89–605 (of fundamental importance, with numerous illustrations; *atrium, RBK* 1, 421–40; *CIAC*, 505–58; *balconies, RBK* II, 129–44; *bema, RBK* I, 583–99; *apse, RBK* I, 246–8; *crypt, RBK* V, 454–84.

Furnishings: R.Kautzsch, *Kapitellstudien*, 1936 (still basic); T.Ulbert, *Studien zur dekorativen Reliefplastik des östlichen Mittelmeerraumes. Schranken-platten des 4. bis 11. Jhs.*, 1969; id., *Istanbuler Mitteilungen* 19/20, 1969/70, 339–357 (barrier panels); B.Brenk, *SBK* I, 75–79 (basins for holy water); P.H.F.Jakobs, *Die frühchristlichen Ambone Griechenlands*, 1987; *Milion* 2, 1990, 265–342 (A.Guiglia Guidobaldi, capitals in St Catharine's Monastery); E.Russo, *Sculture del complesso eufrasiano di Parenzo*, 1991; U.Peschlow, in *Armos. Timetikos Tomos ston N.K.Moutsopoulo* III, 1991, 1449–75 (templon in Constantinople); F.Guidobaldi et al., *San Clemente. La scultura del VI secolo*, 1992; *Syrien 1993*, 224, diag.16 (basin for holy water); C.Strube, *Baudekoration im Nordsyrischen Kalksteinmassiv*, 1993; N.Duval and E.Marin, *Salona I. Catalogue de la sculpture architecturale paléochrétienne de Salone*, 1994; J.Kramer, *Korinthische Pilasterkapitelle in Kleinasien und Konstantinopel*, 1994; T.Zollt, *Kapitellplastik Konstantinopels vom 4. bis 6. Jh.*, 1994; R.Warland, *Jahrbuch deutsch. Arch. Instituts* 109, 1994, 371–85 (ambo); *RBK* I, 111–20 (altar); 126–33 (ambo); 900–31 (screen panels); 1055–65 (ciborium).

Export of architectural items: G.Kapitän, *CR* 1980, 71–136 (find at Marzamemi, Sicily); D.Claude, in *Estudios en Homenaja a Don C.Sánchez Albornoz* II, 1984, 55–64; J.-P.Sodini, 'Le commerce des marbres à l'époque protobyzantine', in *Hommes et Richesses dans l'Empire Byzantin*, 1989, 163–86; C.Barsanti, *Rivista dell'Istituto Nazionale d'Archeologia e Storia dell'Arte* 12, 1990, 91–220 (western Black Sea area); R.M.Bonacasa Carra, *Quaderni di Archeologia della Libia* 15, 1992, 307–24 (Sabratha, Libya).

(e) *Forms of church buildings in the provinces of the Empire: general:* Brenk 1977, chapters on the individual regions; Deichmann 1983, 236–88; Krautheimer 1986, 68, 92, 93–199.

Rome: R.Krautheimer et al., *Corpus Basilicarum Christianarum Romae I–V*, 1937–77; Brandenburg (see above 1 a); F.Tolotti, *RM* 89, 1982, 152–212 (ambulatory basilicas); R.Krautheimer, *Rom. Schicksal einer Stadt 312–1308*, 1987; Arbeiter (see above, 1 a); H.A.Stützer, *Frühchristliche Kunst im Rom*, 1991, 67–175. *Milan: Milano 1990*, 115–48; S.Storz, in *Bautechnik der Antike*, 1991, 224–37 (S.Lorenzo). *Ravenna:* F.W.Deich-mann, *Frühchristliche Bauten und Mosaiken von Ravenna*, 1958; id., *Ravenna – Hauptstadt des spätantiken Abendlandes* I–III, 1974–89; P.Grossmann, *S.Michele in Africisco zu Ravenna*, 1973; L.von Matt and G.Bovini, *Ravenna*, 1979; H.A.Stützer, *Ravenna und seine Mosaiken*, 1989.

Balkans: R.F.Hoddinott, *Early Byzantine Churches in Macedonia and Southern Serbia*, 1963; G.Koch, *Albanien*, 1989, 30–46 (with bibliography); *CIAC*, 2345–88 (Slovenia, Istria); 2389–440 (Dalmatia); 2441–62 (Serbia, Montenegro); 2463–78 (Heracleia); 2491–559 (Bulgaria); 2561–615

(Roumania); 2517–656 (Albania); D.Basler, *Spätantike und frühchristliche Architektur in Bosnien und der Herzegowina*, 1993; S.Anamali, *CR* 1993, 44–74 (Albania); J.Jelicic-Radonic, *Gata. A Church from Justinian's Time*, 1994; id., *Early Christian Twin Churches in Stari Grad on the Island of Hvar*, 1994; J.Belamaric et al., *Early Christian Monuments on the Island of Brac*, 1994. *Greece*: *RBK* II, 1121–41; D.Pallas, *Les monuments paléochrétiens de Grèce découverts de 1959 à 1973*, 1977; *CIAC*, 2687–711; *CR* 1991 (several articles on the Cyclades and Crete). *Crimea*: *RBK* V, 375–99; *Georgia*: *RBK*, 662–76; R.Mepisaschwili and W.Zinzadse, *Georgien. Kirchen und Wehrbauten*, 1987; L.-G. Krouchkova, *Byzantion* 59, 1989, 88–127; *CIAC*, 2657–86. *Armenia*: *RBK* I, 306–16; F.Gandolfo, *Le basiliche Armene, IV–VII sec.*, 1982; J.-M.Thierry, *Armenische Kunst*, 1988.

Constantinople, Asia Minor: T.F.Mathews, *The Early Churches of Constantinople*, 1971; *RBK* I, 690–719 (Binbir Kilisse); II, 164–207 (Ephesus), 1203–23 (Hierapolis); Müller-Wiener 1977, 72–78, 84, 98, 112, 122, 147–52, 186–7, 190–2; M.Restle, *Studien zur frühbyzantinischen Architektur Kappadokiens*, 1979; H.Hellenkemper and F.Hild, *Neue Forschungen in Kilikien*, 1986; W.Müller-Wiener, *SBK* I, 13–20 (Constantinople); O.Feld, *SBK* I, 77–86 (Hierapolis Kastabala); *CIAC*, 1563–619; M.Harrison, *Ein Tempel für Byzanz*, 1990 (Hagios Polyeuktos); *RBK* IV, 182–356 (southern and south–eastern Turkey); 366–96 (Constantinople); S.Möllers, *Die Hagia Sophia in Iznik/Nikaia*, 1994; Painter (see II.1 below), 213–38 (H.Hellenkemper, southern Asia Minor). *Cyprus*: A.H.S.Megaw, *DOP* 28, 1974, 57–88; Pallas (see above under Greece), 267–306; A.Papageorghiou, *CR* 1985, 299–324. *Syria, Mesopotamia*: *RBK* II, 962–1033 (Hauran, southern Syria); III, 852–902 (Qalat Siman, Qalb Louzeh); Grossmann, see below under Ravenna (broad-arcaded basilicas); Wiessner, see above,1 a (Tur Abdin); T.Ulbert, *Resafa II, Die Basilika des Heiligen Kreuzes in Resafa-Sergiupolis*, 1986; C.Strube, *SBK*, 109–23; G.Tchalenko, *Eglises syriennes à bema, texte*, 1990; W.Khouri et al., *AW* 1990.1, 14–25 (northern Syria); *Syrien 1993*, 66–81, 201–55 (general); 82–101 (southern Syria with list of churches), 112–27 (Resafa), 128–43 (Qalat Siman). *Jordan*: *RBK* II, 734–66 (Gerasa); M.Piccirrilo, *Chiese e mosaici della Giordania Settentrionale*, 1981; id., *Madaba, Le chiese e i mosaici*, 1989; *CIAC*, 1697–1736; Painter (see above, II 1), 149–212 (N.Duval).

Palestine: A.Ovadiah, *Corpus of Byzantine Churches in the Holy Land*, 1979; *RBK* I, 601–11 (Bethlehem); III, 588–600 (Jerusalem); R.Rosenthal-Heginbottom, *Die Kirchen von Sobota und die Dreiapsidenkirchen des Nahen Ostens*, 1982; *Christian Archaeology in the Holy Land: New Discoveries. Essays in Honor of V.C.Corbo*, 1990; *CIAC*, 1737–70; Y.Tsafrir (ed.), *Ancient Churches Revealed*, 1993.

Egypt: RBK I, 61–90; *CIAC*, 1843–1908; Grossmann (see 1 g below, Abu Mina); id., 'The Triconchoi in Early Christian Churches of Egypt and their Origins in the Architecture of Classical Rome', in *Roma e l'Egitto nell'Antichità classica*, 1992, 181–90. *Libya:* J.B.Ward Perkins and R.G.Goodchild, *Archaeologia* 95, 1953, 1–83; *CIAC*, 2743–98. *Tunisia, Algeria: RBK* I, 837–66; III, 1158–89 (Carthage); N.Duval, *Les églises africaines à deux absides*, I, II, 1971, 1973; Christern (see 1 g below); W.Gessel, *Monumentale Spuren des Christentums im römischen Nordafrika*, special number of *AW*, 1981; *CIAC*, 1927–60 (cf. 2798–805); 1961–974 (cf. 2805–6); I.Gui et al., *Basiliques chrétiennes d'Afrique du Nord* I, *Inventaire de l'Algérie*, 1992.

Spain: P.de Palol, *Arqueologia Cristiana de la Espana romana*, 1967, 3–103; *RBK* III, 152–205; T.Ulbert, *Frühchristliche Basiliken mit Doppelapsiden auf der spanischen Halbinsel*, 1978; H.Schlunk and T.Hauschild, *Hispania Antiqua. Die Denkmäler der frühchristlichen und westgothischen Zeit*, 1978; *CIAC*, 1975–2027. *France: Naissance des arts chrétiens. Atlas des monuments paléochrétiens de la France*, ed. N.Duval, 1991, 44–93, 184–219. *England:* A.C.Thomas, *Christianity in Roman Britain to AD 500*, 1981; *CIAC*, 2031–72. *Germany: CIAC*, 2077–88; E.Dassmann, *Die Anfänge der Kirche in Deutschland*, 1993, 25–158. *Austria:* R.Egger, *Frühchristliche Kirchenbauten im südlichen Norium*, 1916; *CIAC*, 2089–124; F.Glaser, *Das frühchristliche Pilgerheiligtum auf dem Hemmaberg*, 1991.

(f) *Monasteries: general:* W.Braunfels, *Abendländische Klosterbaukunst*, ⁴1980 (also a brief introduction to the early period); *Les Kellia. Ermitages coptes en Basse-Egypte*, Geneva 1989/90. *Wilderness of Judaea:* Y.Hirschfeld, *The Judean Desert Monasteries in the Byzantine Period*, 1992. *Syria: RBK* II, 976–96; *Syrien 1993*, 66–81. *Alahan Monastir: RBK IV*, 254–63; TIB 5, 193–4 (with further bibliography, especially M.Gough). *Constantinople, Studios Church:* Müller-Wiener 1977, 142–52; *RBK IV*, 373–83.

(g) *Pilgrimage sanctuaries: general:* H.Donner, *Pilgerfahrt ins Heilige Land*, 1979; *SFC*, 211–22 (J.Christern); R.Klein, *RQ* 85, 1990, 145–81 (pilgrimages to Palestine). *Qalat Siman: RBK* III, 853–982; *SFC*, 219–21; *CIAC*, 1675–95; *Syrien 1993*, 128–43. *Resafa: Syrien 1993*, 112–27. *Meriamlik: RBK IV*, 228–39; TIB 5, 441–3. *Abu Mina: RBK* III, 1116–58; *SFC*, 211–18; P.Grossman, *Abu Mina I. Die Gruftkirche und die Gruft*, 1989. *Tebessa:* J.Christern, *Das frühchristliche Pilgerheiligtum von Tebessa*, 1976. *Lechaion: RBK IV*, 769–76. *Thessaloniki, Hagios Demetrios:* G.A.and M.G.Sotirou, *He basilike tou Hagiou Demetriou Thessalonikes*, 1952; C.Bakirtzis, *The Basilica of St Demetrius*, 1988.

2. *Secular architecture*

(a) *City lay-outs*: D.Claude, *Die byzantinische Stadt*, 1969; Deichmann 1983, 265–6; Müller-Wiener 1977, 16–23, 248–70; *RBK* II, 164–6 and passim (Ephesus); III, 687–717 (Justiniana Prima); *Syrien 1993*, 112–27 (Resafa); J.Lauffray, *Halabiyya-Zenobia* I, II, 1983, 1991.

(b) *Public places, forums, triumphal columns and arches, streets: Constantinople*: Müller-Wiener, 1977, 248–67 (forums, columns, arches), 64–71 (obelisk); *RBK* IV, 396–403; U.Peschkow, *SBK* I, 21–33 (triumphal columns); *Trier 1984*, 87f., no.4a (forum); *RBK* III, 687–717 (Justiniana Prima); II, 210f. (Ephesus, 'Arcadian Way' with columns and 'Street of Curetes').

(c) *The fortifications of cities, fortresses: general*: C.Foss and D.Winfield, *Byzantine Fortifications*, 1986. *Constantinople:* Müller-Wiener 1977, 286–319; *RBK* IV, 403–9. *Fortresses:* e.g. F.De Maffei, *CR* 1985, 109–50 (fortifications from the time of Justinian in the East); *Trier 1984*, 322ff., nos.164–70; N.Duval, *CR* 1983, 149–204 (North Africa); *RBK* II, 1004–11 (southern Syria); I.Mikulcic, *CR* 1986, 253–77 (Balkans); G.Koch, *Albanien*, 1989, 34f.; *Milion* 2, 1990, 135–228 (F.de Maffei, Zenobia and Annoukas); 229–264 (E.Zanini, Dara).

(d) *Houses, villas, palaces, hippodromes, bishops' palaces, inns: houses*: R.Stilwell, *DOP* 15, 1961, 47–57 (Antioch); S.Eyice, *Milion* 1, 1988, 15–57 (Cilicia); *RBK* II, 933–1003; *Syrien 1993*, 102–11 (southern Syria); *AS*, 359–62, nos.337–8 (Ephesus, private houses; Ostia); A.Karivieri, in *Post-Herulian Athens*, ed.P.Castrén, 1994, 115–39 (Athens). *Villas: Trier 1984*, 286ff., no.151 (Welschbillig); 310ff., no.161 (Konz); 319ff., no.163 (Palatiolum-Pfalzel); *RBK* IV, 306–8, S.Eyice, *SBK* I, 63–76 and *TIB* 5, 165–6 (Ak Kale, Turkey); *AS*, 115ff., nos.104 (Split), 105 (Piazza Armerina); J.J.Wilkes, *Diocletian's Palace, Split*, 1986; A.Carandini et al., *Filosofiana. La villa di Piazza Armerina*, 1982; *Milano 1992*, 147–56. *Private palaces*: Müller-Wiener 1977, 122–5, 238–42; *RBK* IV, 417–18 (Lausus, Antiochus and Bodum palaces in Constantinople). *Ephesus: RBK* II, 202–4. *Sirmium, Romuliana, etc.*: D.Srejovic, *Roman Imperial Towns and Palaces in Serbia*, 1993. *Imperial palace and hippodrome in Constantinople:* Müller-Wiener 1977, 64–71, 229–37; *RBK* IV, 209–17. *'Basilika' and other parts of the palace in Trier: Trier 1984*, 139ff., no 52b. Milan: *Milano 1990*, 99 nos.2a, 8, 324–31, 454–5; *Milano 1992*, 137–46 (which brings together all the palaces). *Antioch: RBK* I, 190/1. *Ravenna:* Deichmann (see 1 e above, Ravenna), III, 49–75. *Bishops' palaces: RBK* II, 335–71; *CIAC*, 651–709 (and several other articles in the same place, 345–502). *Inns:* e.g. G.Tchalenko, *Villages antiques de la Syrie du Nord* II, 1959, pls.17, 68.

(e) *Aqueducts, cisterns, fountains, baths: general:* R.Tölle-Kastebein, *Antike Wasserkultur,* 1990. *Aqueducts and cisterns: Die Wasserversorgung antiker Städte* II, 1987, 11ff., (Pergamum); III, 1988, 84ff. (Cologne); *RBK* IV, 314–17 (aqueducts and cisterns in Cilicia); W.Brinker, *Damascener Mitteilungen* 5, 1991, 119–48 (Resafa). *Constantinople:* Müller-Wiener 1977, 48–51 (baths), 273–7 (aqueduct of Valens), 278–85 (cisterns). *Fountains:* W.Jobst, *SBK* I, 47–62 (Ephesus). *Baths:* I.Bielsen, *Thermae et Balnea. The Architecture and Cultural History of Roman Public Baths,* ²1993; *Trier 1984,* 199 no.85 (imperial baths); *AS* 358f., no.336 (Scholasticia baths, Ephesus).

(f) *Market basilicas, shops, granaries, oil presses: basilicas:* Müller-Wiener 1977, 248, 258 (Senate curia, basilica on the Theodosius forum). *Shops:* S.Crawford, *The Byzantine Shops at Sardis,* 1990. *Granaries:* G.Rickman, *Roman Granaries and Store Buildings,* 1971; J.Borchhardt et al., *Myra. Eine lykische Metropole,* 1975, 66–71 (Andriake); *Trier 1984,* 200–2, no.88; *Milano 1990,* 102/3, nos.2a, 10; 462 (Milan); *Monumenta Asiae Minoris Antiqua* III, 1921, 104f., diag. 137 (Korasion). *Oil presses:* O.Callot, *Huileries antiques de Syrie du Nord,* 1984. *Trunk roads, bridges: bridges:* numerous references in Procopius, *De aed.,* e.g. V 5; C.O'Connor, *Roman Bridges,* 1993; *Trier 1984,* 93 no.13; *TIB* 5, 154 (Adana), 352 (Mopsuestia), 436 (Tarsus); W.Wurster and J.Ganzert, *Archäol. Anzeiger* 1978, 288–307 (Limyra); Brenk 1977, pl.130 (Sangarius)

III. Burials

On catacombs and tombs generally: P.Styger, *Römische Katakomben,* 1933; id., *Römische Märtyrergrüfte,* 1935; P.Testini, *Le catacombe e gli antichi cimiteri cristiani in Roma,* 1966; *RBK* II, 192–8 (Ephesus, Necropolis of the Seven Sleepers); J.M.C.Toynbee, *Death and Burial in the Roman World,* 1971; E.Kirschbaum and E.Dassmann, *Die Gräber der Apostelfürsten,* 1974; *Beth She'arim* II, III, 1974, 1976; J.Fink, *Die römischen Katakomben,* special number of *AW,* 1978; J.Stevenson, *Im Schattenreich der Katakomben,* 1980; E.Dinkler, *Gymnasium* 87, 1980, 1–37 (Peter and Paul in Rome); Deichmann 1983, 46–53, 57–67; H.A.Stützer, *Die Kunst der römischen Katakomben,* 1983; id., *Frühchristliche Kunst im Rom,* 1991, 7–66; H.Brandenburg, in *Vivarium. Festschrift T.Klauser,* 1984, 11–49 (origin of the catacombs); F.Tolotti, *Rivista di Archeologia Cristiana* 60, 1984, 122–61 (Triclia under S.Sebastiano, Rome); L.Reekmans, *Boreas* 7, 1984, 242–60 (catacombs); id., *SBK* II, 11–37 (hypogea); Effenberger 1986, 24–34, 38–47; Krautheimer 1986, see index (Grabbauten Rom, Ravenna, etc.); H.von Hesberg, *Römische Grabbauten,* 1992; H.G.Thümmel, *Boreas* 16,

1993, 97–113 (memorial of Peter; on the veneration of martyrs generally); *Syrien 1993*, 232ff. pls.29, 50 (El Bara). *Chamber tombs*, see IV.1. *Ravenna, Galla Placidia and Centcelles*: see II 1 e and IV 2. *Rome, S.Costanza*, see II.1. *On individual catacombs*: J.G.Deckers et al., *Die Katakombe 'Santi Marcellino e Piettro'*, 1987; ead., *Die Katakombe 'Anonima di Via Anapo'*, 1991; ead., *Die Katakombe 'Commodilla'*, 1994. There is a list of catacombs in and outside Rome in *Enciclopedia dell'Arte Antica* II, 1959, 416–32.

IV. Paintings and Mosaics

General: H.Koch, *Die altchristliche Bilderfrage*, 1917; W.Elliger, *Die Stellung der alten Christen zu den Bildern in den ersten vier Jahrhunderten*, 1930; T.Klauser, *Gesammelte Arbeiten zur Liturgiegeschichte, Kirchengeschichte und Christlichen Archäologie*, *JbAChr*, supplementary volume 3, 1974, 328–37 (early church statements on art), 338–46 (reflections on the origin of early Christian art); Deichmann 1983, 109–66; *SFC*, 223–40 (D.Stutzinger); Effenberger 1986, 47–51; Thümmel 1992; *RBK* I, 616–62 ('Bild', K.Wessel).

1. *Wall paintings (and mosaics)*: J.Wilpert, *Die Malereien der Katakomben Roms*, I–II; id., *Die römischen Mosaiken und Malereien der kirchlichen Bauten vom 4.bis 13.Jh.*, 1916, partial reprint with supplements, J.Wilpert and W.N.Schumacher, *Die römischen Mosaiken der kirchlichen Bauten vom 4.bis 13. Jahrhundert*, 1976;

G.Matthiae, *Pittura romana del medioevo*, 1965; Kraeling, see above, II 1 a (Dura Europos); U.Fasola, *Le catacombe di S.Gennaro a Capodimonte*, 1975; L.Kötzsche-Breitenbruch, *Die neue Katakombe an der Via Latina*, 1976; V.M.Strocka, *Die Wandmalereien der Hanghäuser in Ephesos*, Forschungen in Ephesos VIII 1, 1977; Brenk 1977, pls. 44–67, 134–5, 146, 222, 289–91, 385; H.Mielsch, *RM* 85, 1978, 151–207; *AS* 273f., no.250 (Alexandria); E.Simon, *Die konstantinischen Deckengemälde in Trier*, 1986; E.Makre, in *Christianike Thessalonike*, 1990, 169–94 (tombs in Thessalonike); N.Gkioles, *Palaiochristianike techne. Mnemaike zographike*, 1991, e.g. pls. 101–12, 117, 121–5; A.Nestori, *Repertorio topografico delle pitture delle catacombe Romane*, ²1993; C.Ihm, *Die Programme der christlichen Apsismalerei vom 4. bis zur Mitte des 8.Jhs.*, ²1993, cf. Ch.III.

2. *Wall mosaics* (see also IV and IV.1): O.Perler, *Die Mosaiken der Juliergruft im Vatikan*, 1953; H.P.L'Orange and P.J.Nordhagen, *Mosaik. Von der Antike bis zum Mittelalter*, 1960; W.Oakeshott, *Die Mosaiken von*

Rom, 1967; F.B.Sear, *Roman Wall and Vault Mosaics*, 1977; Brenk 1977 (with a bibliography on most of the places mentioned); *AS*, 522f., no.467 (tomb of the Julians); J.Deckers, *JbAChr* 25, 1982, 116–20, diag.9, pl.1c–d (Cologne); *Trier 1984*, 149f., no 56b (Trier 'basilica'); 163f., no.62 (Trier cathedral); H.Schlunk, *Die Mosaikkupel von Centcelles*, 1988; Deichmann (see above, II 1 e, Ravenna); Hellenkemper-Hild (see above, II 1 e, Asia Minor), 120–2 (church in Cilicia); C.Bertelli, *Die Mosaiken*, 1989; Berlin 1992, 138–31, no.47; Byzantium 1994, 80–82, no.73 (S.Michele in Africisco, Ravenna).

3. *Wall-coverings in panel mosaics*: E.Nash, *Bildlexikon zur Topographie des antiken Rom* I, 1961, 190–5 ('Basilica' of Junius Bassus); G.Becati, *Scavi di Ostia VI. Edificio con opus sectile fuori Porta Maria*, 1969; L.Ibrahim et al., *Kenchreai. Eastern Port of Corinth II. The Panels of Opus Sectile in Glass*, 1976; Brenk 1977, pls.40–4; P.Asemakopolou-Atzaka, *He techne opus sectile sten entoichia diakosmese*, 1980; *Trier 1984*, 163f., no.62 (Trier cathedral); H.Mielsch, *Buntmarmore aus Rom im Antikenmuseum Berlin*, 1985; *Milano 1990*, 133f., no.2a, 28b (Milan); cf. also Cologne 1983, 34 no.11 (Corning, cf. also nos.9–10).

4. *Floors with tesselated and panel mosaics*: D.Levi, *Antioch Mosaic Pavements*, 1957; L.Budde, *Antike Mosaiken in Kilikien* I–II, 1969, 1972; H.Kier, *Der mittelalterliche Schmuckfussboden unter besonderer Berücksichtigung des Rheinlandes* (1970, a good introduction also to floors of the early Christian period; Aachen, Cologne); S.Pelekanides and P.I.Atzaka, *Syntagma ton palaiochristianikon psephidoton dapedon tes Hellados* I, 1974; P.Asemakopoulou-Atzaka, *Syntagma...*, II, 1987; G.Akerström-Hougen, *The Calendar and Hunting Mosaics of the Villa of the Falconer in Argos*, 1974; Brenk 1977, e.g. pl.39 (Aquileia), 136a (Mopsuestia), 296 (El Asnam); *AS* 129, diag.18 (Hinton St Mary); J.Deckers, *JbAChr* 25, 1982, 116–20, diag. 8., pls.1a–b (Cologne); F.Guidobaldi et al., *Pavimenti marmorei di Roma dal IV a IX secolo*, 1983; U.Peschlow, in *Beiträge zum Altertumskunde Kleinasiens, Festschrift K.Bittel*, 1983, 435–47; *Trier 1984*, 145–9, nos. 55–6; W.A.Daszeweski, *Dionysos der Erlöser. Griechische Mythen im spätantiken Cypern*, 1985, also: J.G.Deckers, *RQ* 81, 1986, 145–762; Mielsch, *Buntmarmore* (see 3 above); R.and A.Ovadiah, *Hellenistic, Roman and Early Byzantine Mosaic Pavements in Israel*, 1986, e.g. 18ff., no.17, pls.1–12 (Jonah); *Byzantinische Mosaiken aus Jordanien* (Exhibition 1986–88); P.Donceel-Voute, *Les pavements des églises byzantines de Syrie et du Liban*, 1988, e.g. 105, diag. 71; 489, diag. 456 (Adam); W.Jobst and H.Vetters,

Mosaikforschung im Kaiserpalast von Konstantinopel, 1992; M.Picirillo, *The Mosaics of Jordan,* Amman 1993.

5. *Mosaics as tombstones*: Palol, *Arqueologia* (see II 1 e, Spain); Kier, *Schmuckfussboden* (see 4 above), 48, diag. 71 (Bonn, from Maria Laach); Duval, *La mosaique funéraire dans l'art paléochrétien,* 1976; Brenk 1977, pls.314/15 (Tunisia), 321 (Spain); Schlunk-Hauschild (see above II 1 e, Spain), pls.26–27, 75; colour plate II; F.Bejaoui, in *L'Africa romana* 9, 1992, 329–36; *Syrien 1993,* 267ff., pl.11.

6. *Panel paintings and icons*: K Partasca, *Mumienporträts und verwandte Denkmäler,* 1966; K.Weitzmann, *Die Ikone,* 1978; id., *The Monastery of Saint Catherine at Mount Sinai. The Icons* I, 1976; D.L..Thompson, *Mummy Portraits in the J.Paul Getty Muesum,* 1982 (good brief introduction; the triptych is on 46–51, no.8); *AS,* 551ff., nos 496–8; R.Warland, *Das Brustbild Christi. Studien zur spätantiken und frühbyzantinischen Bildgeschichte,* 1986, 195f. A 2, pls.11, 17 (Rome, Commodilla Catacomb); A 3, pl.26 (Ostia); P.Amato, *De vera effigie Mariae. Antiche icone romane,* 1988 (icons in Rome); Thümmel 1992 (on the problem of early depictions, with translated sources, e.g. Eusebius); *Byzance* 1992, 144f., nos.98–9; *Berlin* 1992, 170f., no.84; M.Kunze et al., *Die Antikensammlung. Staatliche Museen zu Berlin,* 1992, 305f. no 168 (family of Septimius Severus).

7. *The illustration of books: general*: K.Weitzmann, *Illustrations in Roll and Codex. A Study of the Origin and Method of Text Illustrations,* ²1970; *RBK* I, 757–67; id., *Spätantike und frühchristliche Buchmalerei,* 1977; *TRE* VI, 1980, 109–35; O.Pächt, *Buchmalerei des Mittelalters. Eine Einführung,* ²1985; A.Geyer, *Die Genese narrativer Buchillustration,* 1989; K.Weitzmann and H.L.Kessler, *The Frescoes of the Dura Synagogue and Christian Art,* 1990 (relation to book illustration); C.Jacob, *Buchmalerei. Ihre Terminologie in der Kunstgeschichte,* 1991; R.Sörries, *Christlich-antike Buchmalerei im Überblick,* 1993. *On individual manuscripts*: K.Klausberg, *Die Wiener Genesis. Eine kunstwissenschaftliche Bilderbuchgeschichte,* 1984; I.Levin, *The Quedlinburg Itala,* 1985; K.Weitzmann and H.L.Kesler, *The Cotton Genesis,* 1986; P.Sevrugian, *Der Rossano-Codex und die Sinope Fragmente,* 1990; M.Büchsel, *Städel-Jahrbuch* 13, 1991, 29–80 (*inter alia* on the Cotton Genesis); D.H.Wright, *Der Vergilius Vaticanus. Ein Meisterwerk spätantiker Kunst,* 1993; *Byzantium* 1994, 74–9 (Cotton Genesis, canon tables, Cod.Pupur.Petrop.).

V. Sculptures

1. *Sarcophagi, pagan examples*: G.Koch and H.Sichtermannn, *Römische Sarkophage*, 1982; G.Koch, *Sarkophage der römischen Kaiserzeit*, 1993.

(a) *General questions*: G.Wilpert, I *sarcofagi Cristiani antichi*, I–III, 1929–36; F.W.Deichmann and T.Klauser, *Frühchristliche Sarkophage in Bild und Wort*, 1966; id., 'Frühchristliche Sarkophage', in *Handbuch der Archäologie* (forthcoming).

(b) *Rome: Rep.I*, 1967, supplements in: G.Mietke, in *Miscellanea V.Saxer*, 1992, 561–75; H.Brandenburg, *RM* 86, 1979, 439–71 (style); K.Eichner, *JbAChr* 24, 1981, 85–113 (technique); D.Stutzinger, *Die frühchristlichen Sarkophagreliefs aus Rom*, 1982; *SFC*, 318–38 (H.Kaiser-Minn, survey); R.Sörries and U.Lange, *AW*, 1986, 1, 2–22 ('polychrome fragments', colours); U.Lang and R.Sörries, *AW*, 1990, 1, 45–56 (colours).

(c) *Ravenna*: J.Kollwitz and H.Herdejürgen, *Die ravennatischen Sarkophage*, *ASR* VIII 2, 1979; F.W.Deichmann, *Ravenna, Hauptstadt des spätantiken Abendlandes*, III, 1989, 333–46.

(d) *Constantinople*: G.Bovini, *CR*, 1962, 155ff., 179f.; R.Farioli, *CR*, 1983, 205ff.; N.Firatli, *La sculpture byzantine figurée au Musée archéologique d'Istanbul*, 1990; A.Effenberger, in *Grabeskunst der römischen Kaiserzeit*, 1993, 237–59; J.G.Deckers and Ü.Serdaroglu, *JbAChr* 36, 1993, 140–63.

(e) *Provinces, Gaul*: F.Benoit, *Sarcophages paléochrétiennes d'Arles et de Marseille*, 1954; G.Drocourt-Dubreuil, *Saint-Victor de Marseille*, 1989; *Antiquité Tardive* 1, 1993 (several contributions, above all on the sarcophagi of Aquitaine); M.Innerzeel, *Antiquité Tardive* 2, 1994, 233–49. *Rhine-Moselle area*: *Trier 1984*, 46, pl.5; 209f., no.96; 235ff., nos.121, 127–9; A.Spiess, *Kölner Jahrbuch für Vor- und Frühgeschichte* 21, 1988, 311–13, nos.37–8, 42–44. *Spanish peninsula*: Palol, *Arqueologia* (see II 1 e, Spain), 188–319; M.Sotomayor, *Sarcofagos romano-cristianos de Espana*, 1975; Schlunk-Hauschild (see above II 1 e, Spain), pls.6–7, 20, 21.1, 24–5, 30–1, 35, 42–3, 45.

Dalmatia: N.Cambi, *The Good Shepherd Sarcophagus and its Group*, 1994.

Alexandria, Porphyry sarcophagi: R.Delbrueck, *Antike Porphyrwerke*, 1932, 212–27.

2. *Other sculptures, general*: J.Kollwitz, *Oströmische Plastik der theodosian-ische Zeit*, 1941; Firatli (see above, VI 1 c); B.Kiilerich, *Late Fourth Century Classicism in the Plastic Arts*, 1993; N.Hannestad, *Tradition in Late Roman Sculpture*, 1994. *Portraits*: R.H.Stichel, *Die römischen Kaiserstatue am Ausgang der Antike*, 1982; *SFC*, 61–8 (U.Peschlow); H.P.L'Orange, *Das spätantike Herrscherbild von Diokletian bis zu den Konstantin-Söhnen*, 1984;

D.Stutzinger, *JbAChr* 29, 1986, 146–65; R.R.R.Smith, in *Aphrodisias Papers* 2, 1991, 144–67 (philosophers in Aphrodisias); *Milano 1992*, 73–86. *Individual pieces or groups*: M.Guarducci, *Rendiconti della Pontificia Accademia Romana* 47, 1974/75, 163–90 ('Hippolytus'); V.M.Strocka, in *Festgabe H.Vetters*, 1985, 229–32 (Scholasticia, Ephesus); E.Gibson, *The 'Christians for Christians' Inscriptions of Phrygia*, 1978; Sothebys, London, 14 December 1990, lot 425 (tombstones from Phrygia); *AS*, 334ff., no. 314 (mixing bowl, New York); 406ff., nos.362–8 (Cleveland group); Berlin 1992, 105f., no.30 (bowl with figures); 108f., no.32 (relief with throne); 112ff., nos.34–36 (reliefs with Peter, children, chariots); 147, no.60 (Simeon); *Trier 1984*, 286–8 (Welschbillig); Brenk 1977, pls.108 (pedestal of the Theodosius obelisk), 110 (pedestals of Porphyrius), 111 (Theodosius column); M.Harrison, *Ein Temple für Byzanz*, 1990, 108–12 ('icons' from Hagios Polyeuktos). *Reliquaries*: H.Buschhausen, *Die spätrömischen Metallscrinia und frühchristlichen Reliquiare* I, 1971; S.Trolle, *Nationalmuseets Arbejdsmark*, 1973, 63–72; W.Gessel, *Oriens Christianus* 72, 1988, 183–202; G.Koch, in *FS Engemann*, 1991, 237–40; Berlin 1992, 146 no.59; *Syrien 1993*, 229, pl.24; 419–21, nos.46–48. *Marble tables*: J.Dresken-Weiland, *Reliefierte Tischplatten aus theodosianischer Zeit*, 1991; E.Chalki, *Le mense paleocristiane*, 1991; on both, G.Koch, *BJb* 195, 1995. *Inscriptions*: A.Ferrua, *Damasus und die römischen Märtyrer*, 1986; *Monumenta Asiae Minoris Antiqua* VIII, 1962, nos.46, 65, 161, 162, 168, etc. (Konya); C.M.Kaufmann, *Handbuch der altchristlichen Epigraphik*, 1917, pls.1, 3, 15, 44, 46–57, 122, 123, 127, 130, 131, 136, 139, 194, 205 (Rome); pls. 68–74, 174 (Konya); *Trier 1984*, 219–32, nos.110–17; H.Merten, *Die frühchristlichen Inschriften*, 1990 (Trier); *Naissance* (see II 1 e, France), 154–63. *Wooden doors*: G.Jeremias, *Die Holztür der Basilika S.Sabina in Rom*, 1980; Brenk 1977, pls.286/7; *AS* 550f., no.495 (Cairo); *Milano 1990*, 129ff., nos 21, 28a; *Milano 1992*, 117–35 (Milan).

VI. Small-scale Forms of Art

General: J.Engemann, *JbAChr* 15, 1972, 154–73: numerous pieces in the exhibition catalogues: *AS*; *Gallien 1980*; *SFC*; *Munich 1989*; Berlin 1992; Byzantium 1992 and Byzantium 1994, cf. ch.VII. *Before Constantine*: *SFC*, 616, no.208; 625, no.213; Berlin 1992, 69, no.1 (Lampe); Thümmel 1992, 44f. (on Clement of Alexandria); P.C.Finney, *The Invisible God. The Earliest Christians on Art*, 1994.

1. *Ivory (and bone)*: R.Delbrueck, *Die Consulardiptychen und verwandte Denkmäler*, 1929; *RBK* I, 1068–75 (consular diptychs); W.F.Volbach,

Elfenbeinarbeiten der Spätantike und des frühen Mittelalters, ³1976, e.g. nos.55 (Nichomachi and Symmachi; also *AS*, 186ff., nos.165–6; *SFC*, 553ff., no.141), 107 (Brescia), 120 (Pola), 140 (cathedra, Ravenna), 676f., no.251 (Trier ivory); A.Cutler, *The Craft of Ivory*, 1985; J.Engemann, *JbAChr* 30, 1987, 172–86; Byzance 1992, 42–83; Berlin 1992, 132ff. no.48 (pyx), 141f. no.53 (diptych); Byzantium 1994. *Bone:* A.Loberdou-Tsigarida, *Osteina plakidia*, 1986.

2. *Silver*: Exhibitions (see above, I 5): London (1977); Berlin (1978/79); Baltimore (1986), and A.Effenberger, in *FS Engemann*, 1991, 241–7; Byzance 1992, 1090–19; Byzantium 1994; K.J.Shelton, *The Esquiline Treasure*, 1981; A.Effenberger (ed), *Metallkunst von der Spätantike bis zum ausgehenden Mittelalter*, 1982; *AS* 132f., no.110 (Corbridge Lanx); 151, no.130 (Mildenhall); 185f., no.164 (Parabiago) and numerous pieces; H.A.Cahn et al., *Die spätrömische Silberschatz von Kaiseraugst*, 1984; *Munich 1989*, 47ff.; M.Mundell Mango, *AW* 1990, 2, 70–88 (Seuso treasure); *SFC*, 530ff., no.138 (Parabiago); 570, no.171 (reliquary); 654ff., no.228 (Missorium of Theodosius); L.Pirzio Biroli Stefanelli, *L'argento dei romani*, 1991; S.A.Boyd and M.Mundell Mango, *Ecclesiastical Silver Plate in Sixth-Century Byzantium*, 1993; M.Mundell Mango and A.Benetti, *The Sevso Treasure* I, *Journal of Roman Archaeology*, Suppl.12, 1994. *Liturgical utensils*: e.g. *AS*, 592ff. *Spoons*: Bonn 1991, 290–4; S.Häuser, *Spätantike und frühbyzantinische Silberlöffel*, *JbAChr*, supplementary vol.19, 1992. *On the stamps*: E.C.Dodd, *Byzantine Silver Stamps*, 1961; ead., *DOP* 41, 1987, 165–79; Exhibition Berlin 1978/79 (see Ch.VII), 46–53; Boyd and Mango, *Ecclesiastical Silver* (above), 57–63, 203–27.

3. *Gold: jewellery*, e.g. *AS*, 71ff., nos.61–62; 283ff., nos.262–3; 302ff., nos.275–308; *SFC* 424f., no.38; 452, no.60; 557ff., no.162; 680, no.257; Byzance 1992, 126–37; B.Deppert-Lippitz, in *Studia Varia from the J.Paul Getty Museum 1*, Occasional Papers on Antiquity 8, 1993, 107–40; Byzantium 1994. *Pins: Trier 1984*, 111ff., no.31 (including 31g, an example with the names of Constantine and Licinius dated 315/16); *Munich 1989*, 72f., no.11 (Maxentius); *Milano 1990*, 45f., nos 1c, 3f, g. *Goblets: AS* 178 no.156; J.Werner, *Der Schatzfund von Vrap in Albanien*, 1986, 12f., nos.1–4. *Reliquaries*, Buschhausen, *Metallscrinia* (see ch.V.2). *Enamel*: G.Haseloff, *Email im frühen Mittelalter*, 1990.

4. *Bronze*, general: D.Bénazeth, *L'art du métal au début de l'ère chrétienne*, 1992; Byzance 1992, 120–5; Byzantium 1994. *Pins, girdle fasteners, reliquary fasteners, etc*: Trier 1984, 298ff., nos. 156–60. *Scales and weights*: N.Franken,

Aequipondia. Figürliche Laufgewichte römischer und frühbyzantinischer Schnell-waagen, 1993. *Lamps: AS* 337ff., nos 3217–21; 620ff., nos.556–61; L.Kötsche, *S B K* III, 45–47; Bénazeth, *L'art du métal*, 109–71. *Caskets:* Buschhausen (see VI.2); E.Dinkler von Schubert, *JbAChr* 23, 1980, 141–57; D.Gaspar, *Römische Kästchen aus Pannonien*, 1986; Bonn 1991, 305–12. *Crosses:* Bénazeth, *L'art du métal*, 173–83. *Containers for incense: AS*, 626f., nos.563–4; C.Billod, *Antike Kunst* 30, 1987, 39–56; I.Richter-Siebels, *Die palästinensischen Weichrauchsgefässe mit Reliefszenen aus dem Leben Christi*, Berlin dissertation 1990; Berlin 1992, 20–13, nos.14–15. *Statuettes: AS*, 19, no.12; 105, no.97; 222f., no.199; 278f., no.255; 348f., no.331; 571f., no.509; *S F C* 453, no.61; 483f., no.85; 507f., no.114; 586f., no.182. *Bronzes with inlay: AS*, 86ff., nos.76–77; 103f., no.94; 160f., no.137 (= *S F C*, 585, no.181); *Trier 1984*, 196, no.81; Byzantium 1994, 48–50.

5. *Other metals: ampoulles:* A.Grabar, *Ampoules de Terre Sainte (Monza-Bobbio)*, 1958; J.Engemann, *JbAChr* 16, 1973, 5–27; *S F C* 573f., no.173; 696, no.271; L.Kötzsche, in *Vivarium. FS T.Klauser*, *JbAChr* supplementary vol.11, 1984, 229–46. *Measuring jar: S F C* 666ff., no.242.

6. *Glass, general:* Cologne 1988; Bonn 1991, 257ff., *Gilded glass:* J.Engemann, *JbAChr* 16, 1973, 127–9; *AS*, 89f., no.79 (Alexander, Cleveland) and many others; R.Pillinger, *Studien zu römischen Zwischengold-gläsern* I, 1984; Cologne 1988, 25–7; *Munich 1989*, 113f., nos.40–41; Bonn 1991, 263–7; *Milano 1992*, 103–6. *Diatretes: Trier 1984*, 129ff., nos.41–5; Cologne 1988, 25–7, 186–7, 238–49; K.Goethert, *Trierer Zeitschrift* 52, 1989, 353–68; D.Whitehouse, *Journal of Glass Studies* 30, 1988, 28–33; G.D.Scott, *Journal of Glass Studies* 35, 1993, 106–18. *Engraved glass:* G.N.Brands, *JbAChr* 26, 1983, 107–27; Cologne 1988, 179–237; Bonn 1991, 258–89 (good survey of the three main groups). *Mould-blown glass: AS* 386f., nos 354–6; Cologne 1988, 151–77; Byzance 1992, 99 no.53. *Small objects: AS* 289, no.267 (statuette, extant height still 19 cm!); Cologne 1988, 24 no.4 (bust).

7. *Cut stones: R A C* XI, 1979, 270–313 (J.Engemann, very good survey). *Gems: AS* 436ff., nos 393, 395; P.Zazoff, *Die Antiken Gemmen*, 1983, esp.374–86; *S F C*, 430ff., nos.43–4 (imperial gems, Berlin and London); 560f., no.165 (New York); 574 no.174 (Vienna); Byzance 1992, 86f., 35–7. *Magical gems:* Zazoff, *Antiken Gemmen*, 349–62; *S F C* 153–60 (H.Philipp); H.Philipp, *Mira et Magica*, 1986; C.Höcker, *Antike Gemmen. Staatliche Kunstsammlungen Kassel*, 1987/88, 97ff., nos. 94, 95, 102, 104–6 (perhaps from late antiquity); *Munich 1989*, 222–5. *Cameos: R B K* III, 903–8; *R A C*

XI, 1979, 299–306 (J.Engemann, with a discussion of the known examples); *SFC*, 432ff., no 45 (Trier), 46 (Belgrade), 47 (The Hague); cf. also no.48 (Stuttgart, probably not fourth century); *Trier 1984*, 117f., no.184 (with a reference to other pieces); J.Meischner, *Archäol. Anzeiger* 1993, 613–19 ('Wedding Cameo' of Honorius); J.Spier, 'Late Antique Cameos', in *Cameos in Context. The Benjamin Zucker Lectures 1990*, 1993, 42–54. *Statues in the round, vessels: AS* 161, no.315 (New York); 333, no.318 ('Rubens Vase', Baltimore); *Gallien 1980*, 83f., nos.93–7; *Trier 1984*, 118, no.335 (agate scales, Vienna); *Der Schatz von San Marco in Venedig*, 1984, 90ff., no.2 (cf. also nos.3 and 8); *Milano 1990*, 43, nos.1c, 3a (Julian the Apostate?); Byzance 1992, 84f., no.33 (Constantine?).

8. *Textiles: general introduction*: M.-H.Rutschowscaya, *Tissus coptes*, 1990; L.von Wilckens, *Die textilen Künste. Von der Spätantike biz um 1500*, 1991; A.Stauffer, *Spätantike und koptische Wirkereien. Untersuchungen zur ikonographischen Tradition in spätantiken und frühmittelalterlichen Textilwerkstätten*, 1992; *Syrien 1993*, 180–93. *Silk: AS*,462f., no.413; L.Kötzsche, in *Riggisberger Berichte* 1, 1993, 183–94. *Fabric coloured by reserve technique*: V.Illgen, *Zweifarbige reservetechnisch eingefärbte Leinenstoffe mit grossfigurigen biblischen Darstellung aus Ägypten*, Mainz dissertation 1968; *AS*, 433ff., nos.390–2; F.Baratte, *Monuments et Memoirs* 67, 1985, 31–76. *Fabric with nap*: S.Schrenk, in *Riggisberger Berichte* 1, 1993, 167–81. *Painted fabric*: K.Parlasca, *Mumienporträts und verwandte Denkmäler*, 166, 152–92; M.H.Rutschowscaya, *La Peinture Copte. Musée du Louvre*, 1992, 80–6; Byzantium 1994, 80, no.72; L.Kötzsche, *Der Behang mit alttestamentlichen Malereien der Abegg-Stiftung*, 1996. *Tunics*: C.Nauert, *Koptische Textilkunst im spätantiken Ägypten*, 1978 (see 78, Asterius of Amaseia); *AS*, 348f., no.332. *Ikons: AS*, 532f., no.477 (Cleveland); 549f., no.494; Thümmel 1992, 69f. (Epiphanius of Salamis).

9. *Clay, utensils*: e.g.: *Trier 1984*, 332ff. (which also includes goblets in Barbotine technique); V.Deroché, *Recherches sur la céramique byzantine*, 1989; S.Künzl, *Jahrbuch des Museums für Kunst und Gewerbe*, Hamburg, NF 9/10, 1990/91, 43–54; R.Pirling, *Germania* 71, 1993, 387–404. *Lamps*: A.Ennabli, *Lampes chrétiennes de Tunisie*, 1976; *Munich 1989* (numerous examples); Berlin 1992, 69 no.1; M.T.Paleani, *Le lucerne paleocristiane. Monumenti, Musei, Gallerie Ponifice, Antiquarium Romanum*, Cat.1, 1993. *Pilgrim ampoules*: C.Metzger, *Les ampoules à eulogie du Musée du Louvre*, 1981; *SFC*, 575ff., no.175; *Munich 1989*, 161, no.1854; Z.Kiss, *Les ampoules de Saint-Ménas. Alexandrie V*, 1989; Byzance 1992, 156f., no 106; Byzantium 1994, 110–13. *Scales, tablets etc., from North Africa*:

J.W.Salomonson, *Bulletin...Antieke Beschaving* 44, 1969, 4–109; *SFC*, nos.148, 178, 184–6, 201, 204, 215, 259–63; *Munich 1989*, 85ff., 116ff., 159ff.; K.Weidemann, *Spätantike Bilder des Heidentums und Christentums*, 1990; M.Armstrong, *Kölner Jahrbuch für Vor- und Frühgeschichte* 24, 1991, 413–75 (numerous fragments in Cologne); Berlin 1992, 102 no.27. *Pilgrim souvenirs*: C.Jolivet-Lévy et al., *Les saints et leur sanctuaire à Byzance*, 1993, 25–33; L.Y.Rahmani, *Atiqot* 22, 1993, 109–19; Byzantium 1994, 113–15.

10. *Wood*: M.-H.Rutschowscaya, *Musée du Louvre. Catalogue des bois de l'Egypte copte*, 1986; E.Dauterman Maguire et al., *Art and Holy Power in the Early Christian House*, 1989 (various pieces); Berlin 1992, 166ff., nos.81–82, 83 (wooden casket), 95–103; L.von Matt, *Die Kunstsammlungen der Biblioteca Apostolica Vaticana Rom*, 1969, 171, pls.66–67; *Ornamenta Ecclesiae. Kunst und Künstler der Romanik* III, 1985, 80f., no.H8; *Splendori di Bisanzio. Ravenna*, 1990, 140f., no.52 (wooden casket in the Vatican). For the wooden doors see V 2.

11. *Coins and contorniates*: *general introduction to numismatics*: M.R.Alföldi, *Antike Numismatik* 1978. *Coins from late antiquity*: J.P.C.Kent et al., *Die römische Münze*, 1973, 58ff.; *Munich 1989*, 27ff., 90ff.; P.Grierson and M.Mays, *Catalogue of Late Roman Coins in the Dumbarton Oaks Collection. From Arcadius and Honorius to the Accession of Anastasios*, 1992. *The Noah coins from Apameia Kibotos*: *AS*, 383, no.350. *Constantine's medallion with the Christogram*: *AS*, 66, no.57; *SFC*, 639ff., no.224; *Munich 1989*, 107ff., no. M.145; Lactantius, *De mortibus persecutorum* 44.5; Eusebius, *Vita Constantini* I, 28–31. *Contorniates*: A. and E.Alföldi, *Die Kontorniat-Medaillons* I, 1976, II, 1990; *SFC* 70–4 (B.Kleer).

IX

Abbreviations

Krautheimer 1988	R.Krautheimer, *Ausgewählte Aufsätze zur europäischen Kunstgeschichte*, 1988
Milano 1990	*Milano capitale dell'impero romano 286–402 dc*, 1990
Milano 1992	*Felix Temporis Reparatio. Milano capitale dell'impero romano*, ed. G.Sena Chiesa and E.A.Arslan, 1992
Müller–Wiener 1977	W.Müller–Wiener, *Bildlexikon zur Topographie Istanbuls*, 1977
Munich 1989	*Spätantike zwischen Heidentum und Christentum. Prähistorische Staatssammlung München*, by J.Garbsch and B.Overbeck, 1989
RBK	*Reallexikon zur byzantinischen Kunst* 1ff., 1966ff.
Rep.I	F.W.Deichmann et al., *Repertorium der christlichantiken Sarkophage* I, *Rom und Ostia*, 1967
RM	Mitteilungen des Deutschen Archäologischen Instituts, Römische Abteilung 1ff., 1886ff.
RQ	*Römische Quartalschrift* 1ff., 1887ff.
SBK	*Studien zur spätantiken und byzantinischen Kunst, F.W.Deichmann gewidmet* I–III, 1986
SFC	*Spätantike und frühes Christentum. Liebieghaus, Museum alter Plastik*, Frankfurt 1983
Syrien 1993	*Syrien. Von den Aposteln zu den Kalifen*, Linz, etc., introduction by E.M.Rupprechtsberger 1993
Thümmel 1992	H.G.Thümmel, *Die Frühgeschichte der ostkirchlichen Bilderlehre*, 1992
TIB 5	F.Hild and H.Hellenkemper, *Kilikien und Isaurien*, Tabula Imperii Byzantini 5, 1990
Trier 1984	*Trier – Kaiserresidenz und Bischofssitz. Die Stadt in spätantiker und frühchristlicher Zeit*, 1984

Sources of Illustrations

Author, pls.6–10; 12.2; 13.2–4; 14.2–3; 17.2; 22–23; 24.1; 25.2–3; 26; 27.3; 30.1.

Berlin, Museum für Spätantike und Byzantinische Kunst, pls.31.2; 32.1.

Deutsches Archäologisches Institut, Rom, pls.2–5; 12.1; 13.1; 14.1; 15; 17.1; 18.2; 19.1,3; 20.1; 21.2; 24.2–3; 25.1; 27.1–2; 29.2; 31.3; 32.3.

Deutsches Archäologisches Institut, Istanbul, pls.28.1–2.

Marburg, Christliches Archäologisches Seminar, pls.1; 11; 18.1; 19.2; 20.2; 21.1; 28.3; 29.1; 30.2; 30.4; 31.1.

Munich, Bayerisches Nationalmuseum, pl.30. 3.

Munich, Staatliche Münzsammlung, pl.32. 4.

Rome, Pontificia Commissione di Archeologia Sacra, pl.16

Trier, Rheinisches Landesmuseum, pls. 29.3; 32.2.

X

Postscript

The present volume is an 'introduction' to the architecture and art of the early Christian period, not a 'history of early Christian art'. Within the given length of the book and the limited number of line drawings and plates, as many aspects as possible have been considered, and the texts are correspondingly brief. Of course disputed views cannot be discussed in so short a book.

The extended bibliographies will make it possible to investigate individual problems; they focus on books which should be available in university and other major libraries.

The line drawings have been simplified to match the format of the book; the concern has been more to bring a monument to life than to reproduce all its details.

Special thanks are due to Rosemarie Berghöfer, who put the text on to PC with great care; to Karin Kirchhainer, Heidemarie Koch and Susanne Küther, who read the texts through critically and provided many additions; and Heidemarie Koch who, despite her own urgent work and many other duties, prepared a series of line drawings.

The book is dedicated to my students in Göttingen (1972–1984) and Marburg (from 1979).

J.Schneider suggested the book; I am grateful to him and his colleagues at Kohlhammer Verlag, especially Marlies Rehermann, for their good collaboration and careful production.

Marburg   Guntram Koch

Index